Garnet Poems

garnet

A DRIFTLESS CONNECTICUT SERIES BOOK

This book is a 2012 selection in the Driftless Connecticut Series, for an outstanding book in any field on a Connecticut topic or written by a Connecticut author.

AN ANTHOLOGY OF

CONNECTICUT POETRY

SINCE 1776

poems

EDITED BY DENNIS BARONE

WITH A FOREWORD BY DICK ALLEN

Wesleyan University Press ~ Middletown, Connecticut

Wesleyan University Press
Middletown CT 06459
www.wesleyan.edu/wespress

Manufactured in the United States of America
Designed by Mindy Basinger Hill
Typeset in 10/14 pt. Calluna

THE DRIFTLESS CONNECTICUT SERIES is funded by the Beatrice Fox Auerbach Foundation Fund at the Hartford Foundation for Public Giving.

NATIONAL ENDOWMENT FOR THE ARTS
A great nation deserves great art.

This project is supported in part by an award from the National Endowment for the Arts.

Library of Congress Cataloging-in-Publication Data

Garnet poems: an anthology of Connecticut poetry since 1776 / edited by Dennis Barone.
p. cm.—(Garnet books)
Includes index.
ISBN 978-0-8195-7309-4 (cloth : alk. paper)—
ISBN 978-0-8195-7310-0 (ebook)
"A Driftless Connecticut series book"—T.p. verso.
1. American poetry—Connecticut.
2. Connecticut—Poetry. I. Barone, Dennis.
PS548.C8G37 2012
811'.60809746—dc23 2012010190

5 4 3 2 1

Contents

Foreword

In a United States of America jigsaw puzzle, the state of Connecticut is small and shaped rather like an ordinary rectangle. On the nation's poetry map, however, Connecticut looms large.

Connecticut's importance is made clear by editor Dennis Barone's splendid new anthology, *Garnet Poems: An Anthology of Connecticut Poetry Since 1776*. I once thought of editing a similar anthology myself, and even began gathering poems, but frankly I became worn down with slogging through the extensive works of the Connecticut Wits—historically important but tedious to the modern ear, or at least to me. What a debt we owe to Dr. Barone for his judicious selection from their enterprises.

Other early Connecticut poets are here also, poets one may have heard about but whose work has remained unfamiliar to our times. There's a sample, for instance, of the once famous Lydia Sigourney's verse, popular two centuries ago. And few know that Harriet Beecher Stowe, in her time, was recognized for her poems as well as for *Uncle Tom's Cabin*.

Garnet Poems also reinforces the importance of Connecticut poets in the recent twentieth century. Included are poets undoubtedly among the great Moderns and Contemporaries: West Hartford and Hartford's Wallace Stevens, of course, and also Hamden's Donald Hall, New Haven and Woodbridge's John Hollander, Uncasville and New London's William Meredith, Stonington's James Merrill, Fairfield's Robert Penn Warren, Portland and Middletown's Richard Wilbur and so on.

We're reminded, too, of how poetry that happens to be written by women has come into its own. Dennis Barone's anthology certainly is strong in this regard. It will introduce those not familiar with Connecticut poetry to fifteen fascinating women's voices, including those of nationally honored Marilyn Nelson, Margaret Gibson, Gray Jacobik, and Elizabeth Alexander.

Particularly apt elements of this anthology are the eclectic nature of the selections—from traditional to experimental—and the number of poems that relate to or refer directly to this specific place, this throbbing rectangle *state* of Connecticut.

For Connecticut is at once both a place and more than a physical place. It is the long tidal river, the coastal shore of Long Island Sound, the Barnum parade, the Weir Farm, and the Wadsworth Atheneum, the Sunken Garden Poetry Festival, and the Guilford Poets Guild, while being also a state of mind, a state—if I may be allowed a small play on words—of connections. The land of steady habits consistently gives us poets who think and feel judiciously. They may be Republicans or Democrats or Independents but it seems to me, reading this volume, that they perhaps most often stand off to the side and observe, or, like Wallace Stevens, they imagine differently, or they defend the so-called middle ground.

Their stance and objectivity and freedom of imagination befits a state continually balancing farms, small towns, suburbs, and cities, a state you must cross and recross if you wish to go between the East's great intellectual and artistic hubs of Boston and New York. Many Connecticut poems are metaphorical pauses at places within journeys. *Garnet Poems*, because of space limitations, could not include poems from all of the State's outstanding poets. Ours is a most literary and artistic place and those poets represented here have numerous peers. But this volume should encourage its readers to seek out individual volumes by all. One of the great tasks of an anthology is to whet the appetite and send the reader to bookstores and libraries for full individual poetry volumes. An anthology is a bouquet; a complete book by a given poet is a life.

That said, *Garnet Poems: An Anthology of Connecticut Poetry Since 1776* seems to me indispensable to the understanding and appreciation of Connecticut's and the nation's great literary heritage. Along with Dennis Barone's preface, the poets' short biographies, and a fascinating final note by Dr. Barone, it is a full presentation to the general public of poets past and present. Their work will fit firmly (well, there may be a rough edge or two along the Sound) into the puzzle of ourselves.

DICK ALLEN

Connecticut state poet laureate (2010–2015)

Editor's Preface

A CONNECTICUT TRADITION IN POETRY

Many anthologies beg the question of how their contents have been selected. This book, organized around the state of Connecticut, draws on the work of poets born in the state as well as transplants whose work has become identified with the state. When introducing what might have been the state's first anthology of poetry, *The Poets of Connecticut* (1844), Reverend Charles W. Everest noted that he admitted "the names of none upon our lists who were not born in the commonwealth." Such a method of selection (or exclusion) may have been useful in the mid-nineteenth century, but it cannot prove very useful today. We are—and have been for quite some time—a population ever in flux and on the move.

The poets included in this book have different points of view on their "Connecticut-ness." Some, like Susan Howe, feel the impact of literary forebears. Howe has stated that "as an American poet writing in the early twenty-first century I owe these authors [philosopher-theologian Jonathan Edwards, born in Windsor, Connecticut, and Wallace Stevens] an incalculable debt [. . .] their writing locates, rescues, and delivers what is secret, wild, double, and various in the near at hand." Other writers see frequent rupture due to immigration, industrialization, urbanization, and suburbanization, yet feel the force of the state's culture or climate exerting an influence on their work. The contemporary poet Lewis Turco told me, "It used to bother me a lot that so few poets were actually born in Connecticut. I could never understand how, given the law of averages, that could come to pass. And it bothered me exceedingly that I myself wasn't born there." Turco, born in Buffalo, New York, grew up in Meriden, Connecticut, and attended the University of Connecticut. Charlotte Perkins Gilman, on the other hand, was born here, in Hartford, but resided in California most of her life. Both James Laughlin and Wallace Stevens arrived here from Pennsylvania as transplants and, like the vines intertwined on the state seal and flag, thrived in Connecticut and, in turn, greatly enriched the state.

Wallace Stevens, indisputably the state's greatest poet, was born in Reading, Pennsylvania, and lived a little less than half his life outside of Connecticut. But his nearly forty years' residence and the completion of all his mature work while living in West Hartford and Hartford qualifies him as a Connecticut poet, our quintessential one: "It was evening all afternoon. / It was snowing / And it was going to snow. / The black bird sat / In the cedar-limbs." The more one reads Stevens's poetry, the more one is overwhelmed by its beauty and the intellect of the mind that made it, a mind deeply rooted in Connecticut: its topography, its seasons, its weather.

In the final year of his life Wallace Stevens composed a brief essay about Connecticut for the Voice of America. In it he describes a train ride through the state. "Everything seemed gray, bleached and derelict and the word derelict kept repeating itself as part of the activity of the train. But this was a precious ride through the character of the state. The soil everywhere seemed thin and difficult." The trip through his state leads not to despair but to the conclusion that "we live in the tradition which is the true mythology of the region and we breathe in with every breath the joy of having ourselves been created by what has been endured and mastered in the past." So it is for many Connecticut poets. James Abraham Hillhouse said of his poem "Sachem's Wood" that it is "a testimony of renewed pleasure and pride in my native state."

In his mid-nineteenth-century gathering of poets, Rev. Everest made the claim that "New England has been the nursery of America's literature," and then he added "let the present work determine whether Connecticut has not been its very cradle." Whether or not Connecticut serves as cradle for American poetry seems less important to poets in the early twenty-first century than to poets of prior times who strove to make claims of origin and primacy. We call our age post-modern and post-ethnic and appreciate how the world is in Connecticut and how Connecticut is in the world. An anthology such as *Garnet Poems: An Anthology of Connecticut Poetry Since 1776* provides opportunity to celebrate the art of the present aware of the art of the past.

Connecticut's nickname is The Land of Steady Habits, but the habits of our poets, whether they envision continuity or change, often unsettle the steady, rock the ship of state a bit. In a land so long famous for its weapons manufactories, local poets have written many poems of peace. Connecticut is a land of contradictions. Is Connecticut between the great metropolises of Boston and New York City and hence plump with cosmopolitanism, or might it better be noted that Hartford, the state capital, is halfway between New Haven and Springfield, and hence a tired, old provincialism characterizes this place? Give me the Berlin Turnpike, its neon all aglow and a-glimmering! Or count its barns and working farms, tramp through its glorious network of open land and state hiking trails. In this state that today has the fourth highest population density in the country and that strives to balance an ideal proportion of urban, suburban, and rural, the official projected image turns more often to the bucolic countryside of Bantam than to the gritty downtown of Bridgeport. Poets embrace the mix and write about, as Donald Hall has, "ranch houses stretching flat beyond the square," as well as "the leaves of maples, / reds of seventy different shades, yellow /

like old paper; and poplar leaves, fragile and pale; / and elm leaves." Contradiction is often the impulse in a poem, and can become transformative. Incarnate in the poem, contradictions become magical.

It is also significant that the poets of Connecticut are a very well-educated lot. The first four poets presented in this volume are Yale graduates, and as members of the Connecticut Wits, according to literary historian Vernon L. Parrington, "by their persistent labors in the field of satire they created for the first time in America what may be called a school of poetry." Later, Harriet Beecher Stowe and Charlotte Perkins Gilman were part of the same Connecticut intellectual families. More recent poets have been associated with Yale as well: as faculty, Robert Penn Warren, John Hollander, and Elizabeth Alexander, for example. Connecticut College, Trinity College, and Wesleyan University graduates or professors have made meaningful contributions to poetic Connecticut. Henry Howard Brownell and Chase Twichell graduated from Trinity, for example.

For this anthology I selected several poems or pages of poetry by each poet so that a reader might arrive at a more profound understanding of an artist's work than a single brief poem or excerpt can provide. I selected poems about Connecticut and poems known as a Connecticut author's best writing. Some poems have appeared in other anthologies both past and present. Besides the single-state focus, two other qualities distinguish the present volume. While there are poets in this volume who appear in any and every anthology of American poets—Stevens, for example—there are also a few fine poets who have been long forgotten, such as Anna Hempstead Branch. As an editor moves to the present moment, there is far less editorial precedent or tradition to draw on, and the number of publishing poets increases all the time. Connecticut may be one of the nation's smallest states in square miles, but it is so very rich in poetic achievement. I indicate the breadth and depth of this richness by selecting work evoking a wide aesthetic range: the religious verses of Harriet Beecher Stowe and the battle narratives of Henry Howard Brownell; the prose poems of Russell Edson and the formalism of Richard Wilbur. Lastly, there are some poets represented in *Garnet Poems* who might evoke for a reader another state than this one. Charles Olson, for example, readers immediately associate with Worcester and Gloucester, Massachusetts. Yet Olson began and ended his writing life in Connecticut first at Wesleyan University and then at the University of Connecticut.

I thank Kathleen Kelley of the University of Saint Joseph Library for assistance with interlibrary loans and Ashlee A. Hamilton for assistance in preparing the manuscript. As a practicing poet I thank the poetry publishers of Connecticut, those so vital and necessary for the continuance of the art. Wesleyan University Press has been a national presence in the publishing of poetry since its inception in 1957. The most significant literary publisher in America in the twentieth century, New Directions, led by James Laughlin, maintained an office in Norfolk beginning in 1936. And Yale University Press began its Yale Series of Younger Poets in 1919. It is the oldest program of its kind in the United States. Important recent and current poetry publishers of note include Curbstone Press, Plinth Books, and Potes & Poets Press. Finally, I thank Suzanna Tamminen and the staff of Wesleyan University Press. Suzanna Tamminen and I first discussed this project one late autumn day in Hartford, only a half mile or so from the former home of Wallace Stevens. We felt the poetic aura of Connecticut, the spell of this land on the poetic habits of its writers. May you feel and know this, too.

DENNIS BARONE

Garnet Poems

from Progress of Dulness

Next see our youth at school appear,
Procured for forty pounds a year;
His ragged regiment round assemble,
Taught, not to read, but fear and tremble.
Before him, rods prepare his way,
Those dreaded antidotes to play.
Then throned aloft in elbow chair,
With solemn face and awful air,
He tries, with ease and unconcern,
To teach what ne'er himself could learn;
Gives law and punishment alone,
Judge, jury, bailiff, all in one;
Holds all good learning must depend
Upon his rod's extremest end,
Whose great electric virtue's such,
Each genius brightens at the touch;
With threats and blows, incitements pressing,
Drives on his lads to learn each lesson;
Thinks flogging cures all moral ills,
And breaks their heads to break their wills.
The year is done; he takes his leave;
The children smile; the parents grieve;
And seek again, their school to keep,
One just as good and just as cheap.

. . . .

But ah! How short the fairest name
Stands on the slippery steep of fame!
The noblest heights we're soonest giddy on;
The sun ne'er stays in his meridian;
The brightest stars must quickly set;
And DICK has deeply run in debt.

Not all his oaths can duns dismay,
Or deadly bailiffs fright away;
Not all his compliments can bail,
Or minuets dance him from the jail.
Law not the least respect can give
To the laced coat, or ruffled sleeve;
His splendid ornaments must fall,
And all is lost, for these were all.
  What then remains? In health's decline,
By lewdness, luxury and wine,
Worn by disease, with purse too shallow,
To lead in fashions, or to follow,
The meteor's gaudy light is gone;
Lone age with hasty step comes on.
How pale the palsied fop appears,
Low shivering in the vale of years;
The ghost of all his former days,
When folly lent the ear of praise
And beaux with pleased attention hung
On accents of his chatt'ring tongue.
Now all those days of pleasure o'er,
That chatt'ring tongue must prate no more.
From every place, that blessed his hopes,
He's elbowed out by younger fops.
Each pleasing thought unknown, that cheers
The sadness of declining years,
In lonely age he sinks forlorn,
Of all, and even himself, the scorn.
  The coxcomb's course were gay and clever,
Would health and money last for ever,
Did conscience never break the charm,
Nor fear of future worlds alarm.
But oh, since youth and years decay,
And life's vain follies fleet away,
Since age has no respect for beaux,
And death the gaudy scene must close—
Happy the man, whose early bloom
Provides for endless years to come;

That learning seeks, whose useful gain
Repays the course of studious pain;
Whose fame the thankful age shall raise,
And future times repeat its praise;
Attains that heart-felt peace of mind,
To all the will of HEAVEN resigned,
Which calms in youth, the blast of rage,
Adds sweetest hope to sinking age,
With valued use prolongs the breath,
And gives a placid smile to death.

from M'Fingal

"Brethren and friends, the glorious band
Of loyalty in rebel land!
It was not thus you've seen me sitting,
Return'd in triumph from town-meeting;
When blust'ring Whigs were put to stand,
And votes obey'd my guiding hand,
And new commissions pleased my eyes;
Blest days, but ah, no more to rise!
Alas, against my better light,
And optics sure of second-sight,
My stubborn soul, in error strong,
Had faith in Hutchinson too long.
See what brave trophies still we bring
From all our battles for the king;
And yet these plagues, now past before us,
Are but our entering wedge of sorrows!
"I see, in glooms tempestuous, stand
The cloud impending o'er the land;
That cloud, which still beyond their hopes
Serves all our orators with tropes;
Which, though from our own vapors fed,
Shall point its thunders on our head!
I see the Mob, beflipp'd at taverns,
Hunt us, like wolves, through wilds and caverns!
What dungeons open on our fears!
What horsewhips whistle round our ears!
Tar, yet in embryo in the pine,
Shall run on Tories' backs to shine;
Trees, rooted fair in groves of sallows,
Are growing for our future gallows;
And geese unhatch'd, when pluck'd in fray,
Shall rue the feathering of that day.
"For me, before that fatal time,
I mean to fly th' accursed clime,
And follow omens, which of late
Have warn'd me of impending fate.
"For late in visions of the night
The gallows stood before my sight;

I saw its ladder heaved on end;
I saw the deadly rope descend,
And in its noose, that wavering swang,
Friend Malcolm hung, or seem'd to hang.
How changed from him, who bold as lion,
Stood Aid-de-camp to Gen'ral Tryon,
Made rebels vanish once, like witches,
And saved his life, but dropp'd his breeches.
I scarce had made a fearful bow,
And trembling asked him, "How d'ye do;"
When lifting up his eyes so wide,
His eyes alone, his hands were tied;
With feeble voice, as spirits use,
Now almost choak'd by gripe of noose;
  "Ah, fly my friend, he cried, escape,
And keep yourself from this sad scrape;
Enough you've talked and writ and plann'd;
The Whigs have got the upper hand.
Could mortal arm our fears have ended,
This arm (and shook it) had defended.
Wait not till things grow desperater,
For hanging is no laughing matter.
Adventure then no longer stay;
But call your friends and haste away.

from Greenfield Hill

Rough is thy surface; but each landscape bright,
With all of beauty, all of grandeur dress'd,
Of mountains, hills, and sweetly winding vales,
Of forests, groves, and lawns, and meadows green,
And waters, varied by the plastic hand,
Through all their fairy splendour, ceaseless charms,
Poetic eyes. Springs bubbling round the year,
Gay-wand'ring brooks, wells at the surface full,
Yield life, and health, and joy, to every house,
And every vivid field. Rivers, with foamy course,
Pour o'er the ragged cliff the white cascade,
And roll unnumber'd mills; or like the Nile,
Fatten the beauteous interval; or bear
The sails of commerce through the laughing groves.

With wisdom, virtue, and the generous love
Of learning, fraught, and freedom's living flame,
Electric, unextinguishable, fir'd,
Our Sires established, in thy cheerful bounds,
The noblest institutions, man has seen,
Since time his reign began. In little farms
They measur'd all thy realms, to every child
In equal shares descending; no entail
The first-born lifting into bloated pomp,
Tainting with lust, and sloth, and pride, and rage,
The world around him; all the race beside,
Like brood of ostrich, left for chance to rear,
And every foot to trample. Reason's sway
Elective, founded on the rock of truth,
Wisdom their guide, and equal good their end,
They built with strength, that mocks the battering storm,
And spurns the mining flood; and every right
Dispens'd alike to all. Beneath their eye,
And forming hand, in every hamlet, rose

The nurturing school; in every village, smil'd
The heav'n-inviting church, and every town
A world within itself, with order, peace,
And harmony, adjusted all its weal.

Hence, every swain, free, happy his own lord,
With useful knowledge fraught, of business, laws,
Morals, religion, life, unaw'd by man,
And doing all, but ill, his heart can wish,
Looks round, and finds strange happiness his own;
And sees that happiness on laws depend.
On this heav'n-laid foundation rests thy sway;
On knowledge to discern, and sense to feel,
That free-born rule is life's perennial spring
Of real good. On this alone it rests.
For, could thy sons a full conviction feel,
That government was noxious, without arms,
Without intrigues, without a civil broil,
As torrents sweep the sand-built structure down,
A vote would wipe its every trace away.
Hence too each breast is steel'd for bold defence;
For each has much to lose. Chosen by all,
The messenger of peace, by all belov'd,
Spreads, hence, the truth and virtue, he commends.
Hence manners mild, and sweet, their peaceful sway
Widely extend. Refinement of the heart
Illumes the general mass. Even those rude hills,
Those deep embow'ring woods, in other lands
Prowl'd round by savages, the same soft scenes,
Mild manners, order, virtue, peace, disclose;
The howling forest polish'd as the plain.

. . . .

But chief, Connecticut! on thy fair breast
These splendours glow. A rich improvement smiles
Around thy lovely borders; in thy fields
And all that in thy fields delighted dwell.
Here that pure, golden mean, so oft of yore
By sages wish'd, and prais'd, by Agur's voice
Implor'd, while God th' approving sanctions gave
Of wisdom infinite; that golden mean,
Shines unalloy'd; and here the extended good,
That mean alone secures, is ceaseless found.

. . . .

"My friends, you have my kindest wishes:
Pray think a neighbor not officious,
While thus, to teach you how to live,
My very best advice I give."

"And first, *industrious* be your lives;
Alike employ'd yourselves, and wives:
Your children, join'd in labour gay,
With something useful fill each day.
Those little times of leisure save,
Which most men lose, and all men have;
The half days, when a job is done;
The whole days, when a storm is on.
Few know, without a strict account,
To what these little times amount:
If wasted, while the same your cost,
The sums, you might have earn'd, are lost."

"*Learn small things never to despise:*
You little think how fast they rise.
A rich reward the mill obtains,
'Tho' but two quarts a bushel gains:
Still rolling on its steady rounds,
The farthings soon are turn'd to pounds."

"*Nor think a life of toil severe:*
No life has blessings so sincere.
Its meals so luscious, sleep so sweet,
Such vigorous limbs, such health complete,
A mind so active, brisk, and gay,
As his, who toils the livelong day.
A life of sloth drags hardly on;
Suns set too late, and rise too soon;
Youth, manhood, age, all linger slow,
To him, who nothing has to do.
The drone, a nuisance to the hive,
Stays, but can scarce be said to live,
And well the bees, those judges wise,
Plague, chase, and sting him, 'till he dies.
Lawrence, like him, tho' sav'd from hanging,
Yet every day deserves a banging."

"Let *order* o'er your time preside,
And *method* all your business guide.
Early begin, and end, your toil;
Nor let great tasks your hands embroil.
One thing at once, be still begun,
Contriv'd, resolv'd, pursued, and done.
Hire not, for what yourselves can do;
And send not, when yourselves can go;
Nor, 'till to-morrow's light, delay,
What might as well be done to-day.
By steady efforts all men thrive,
And long by moderate labour live;
While eager toil, and anxious care,
Health, strength, and peace, and life, impair."

"What thus your hands with labour earn,
To save, be now your next concern.
What'er to health, or real use,
Or true enjoyment, will conduce,
Use freely, and *with pleasure* use;
But ne'er the gifts of HEAVEN abuse:
I joy to see your treasur'd stores,
Which smiling Plenty copious pours;
Your cattle sleek, your poultry fine,
Your cider in the tumbler shine,
Your tables, smoking from the hoard,
And children smiling round the board.
All rights to use in you conspire;
The labourer's worthy of his hire.
Ne'er may that hated day arrive,
When worse yourselves, or yours, shall live;
Your dress, your lodging, or your food,
Be less abundant, neat, or good;
Your dainties all to market go,
To feast the epicure, and beau;
But ever on your tables stand,
Proofs of a free and happy land."

. . . .

"*In this New World, life's changing round,*
In three descents, is often found.
The *first*, firm, busy, plodding, poor,
Earns, saves, and daily swells, his store;
By farthings first, and pence, it grows;
In shillings next, and pounds, it flows;
Then spread his widening farms, abroad;
His forests wave; his harvests nod;
Fattening, his numerous cattle play,
And debtors dread his reckoning day.
Ambitious then t' adorn with knowledge
His son, he places him at college;
And sends, in smart attire, and neat,
To travel, thro' each neighbouring state;
Builds him a handsome house, or buys,
Sees him a gentleman, and dies."

"The *second*, born to wealth, and ease
And taught to think, converse, and please,
Ambitious, with his lady-wife,
Aims at a higher walk of life.
Yet, in those wholesome habits train'd,
By which his wealth, and weight, were gain'd,
Bids care in hand with pleasure go,
And blends economy with show.
His houses, fences, garden, dress,
The neat and thrifty man confess.
Improv'd, but with improvement plain,
Intent on office, as on gain,
Exploring, useful sweets to spy,
To public life he turns his eye.
A townsman first, a justice soon;
A member of the house anon;
Perhaps to board, or bench, invited,
He sees the state, and subjects, righted;
And, raptur'd with politic life,
Consigns his children to his wife.
Of household cares amid the round,
For her, too hard the task is found.
At first she struggles, and contends;
Then doubts, desponds, laments, and bends;

Her sons pursue the sad defeat,
And shout their victory complete;
Rejoicing, see their father roam,
And riot, rake, and reign, at home.
Too late he sees, and sees to mourn,
His race of every hope forlorn,
Abroad, for comfort, turns his eyes,
Bewails his dire mistakes, and dies."

"His *heir, train'd only to enjoy,*
Untaught his mind, or hands, t' employ,
Conscious of wealth enough for life,
With business, care, and worth, at strife,
By prudence, conscience, unrestrain'd,
And none, but pleasure's habits, gain'd,
Whirls on the wild career of sense,
Nor danger marks, nor heeds expense.
Soon ended is the giddy round;
And soon the fatal goal is found.
His lands, secur'd for borrow'd gold,
His houses, horses, herds, are sold.
And now, no more for wealth respected,
He sinks, by all his friends neglected;
Friends, who, before, his vices flatter'd,
And liv'd upon the loaves he scatter'd.
Unacted every worthy part,
And pining with a broken heart,
To dirtiest company he flies,
Whores, gambles, turns a sot, and dies.
His children, born to fairer doom,
In rags, pursue him to the tomb."

"Apprentic'd then to masters stern,
Some real good the orphans learn;
Are bred to toil, and hardy fare,
And grow to usefulness, and care;
And, following their great-grandsire's plan,
Each slow becomes a useful man."

“Such here is life’s swift-circling round;
So soon are all its changes found.
Would you prevent th’ allotment hard,
And fortune’s rapid whirl retard,
In all your race, industrious care
Attentive plant, and faithful rear;
With life, th’ important task begin,
Nor but with life, the task resign;
To habit, bid the blessings grow,
Habits alone yield good below.”

A Song

Look, lovely maid, on yonder flow'r,
  And see that busy fly,
Made for the enjoyment of an hour
  And only born to die.

See, round the rose he lightly moves,
  And wantons in the sun,
His little life in joy improves,
  And lives, before 'tis gone.

From this instinctive wisdom, learn,
  The present hour to prize;
Nor leave to-day's supreme concern,
  'Till morrow's morn arise.

Say, loveliest fair, canst thou divine
  That morrow's hidden doom?
Know'st thou, if cloudless skies will shine,
  Or heaven be wrapt in gloom?

Fond man, the trifle of a day,
  Enjoys the morning light,
Nor knows, his momentary play
  Must end, before 'tis night.

The present joys are all we claim;
  The past are in the tomb;
And, like the poet's dream of fame
  The future never come.

No longer then, fair maid, delay
  The promis'd scenes of bliss;
Nor idly give another day,
  The joys assign'd to this.

If *then* my breast can soothe thy care,
  'Twill *now* that care allay;
If joy this hand can yield, my fair
  'Twill yield that joy to-day.

Quit then, oh quit! thou lovely maid,
   Thy bashful, virgin pride;
To-day the happy plot be laid,
   The bands, to-morrow, tied!

The purest joys shall be our own,
   That e'er to man were giv'n;
And those bright scenes, on earth begun,
   Shall brighter shine in heaven.

The Monkey,
Who shaved himself and his Friends

A FABLE

Addressed to the Hon. —— ——.

A MAN who own'd a barber's shop
At York, and shav'd full many a fop,
A monkey kept for their amusement;
He made no other kind of use on't—
This monkey took great observation,
Was wonderful at imitation,
And all he saw the barber do,
He mimic'd straight, and did it too.

It chanc'd in shop, the dog and cat,
While friseur din'd, demurely sat,
Jacko found nought to play the knave in,
So thought he'd try his hand at shaving.
Around the shop in haste he rushes,
And gets the razors, soap, and brushes;
Now puss he fix'd (no muscle miss stirs)
And lather'd well her beard and whiskers,
Then gave a gash as he began—
The cat cry'd "waugh!" and off she ran.

Next Towser's beard he try'd his skill in,
Though Towser seem'd somewhat unwilling:
As badly here again succeeding,
The dog runs howling round, and bleeding.

Nor yet was tir'd our roguish elf;
He'd seen the barber shave himself;
So by the glass, upon the table,
He rubs with soap his visage sable,
Then with left hand holds smooth his jaw,—
The razor in his dexter paw;
Around he flourishes and slashes,
Till all his face is seam'd with gashes.
His cheeks dispatch'd—his visage thin
He cock'd, to shave beneath his chin;
Drew razor swift as he could pull it,
And cut, from ear to ear, his gullet.

MORAL

Who cannot write, yet handle pens,
Are apt to hurt themselves and friends.
Though others use them well, yet fools
Should never meddle with edge tools.

Sonnet I

ADDRESSED TO MY FRIENDS AT YALE COLLEGE, ON MY LEAVING THEM TO JOIN THE ARMY

ADIEU, thou Yale! where youthful poets dwell,
No more I linger by thy classic stream.
Inglorious ease and sportive songs farewell!
Thou startling clarion! break the sleeper's dream!

And sing, ye bards! the war-inspiring theme.
Heard ye the din of battle? clang of arms?
Saw ye the steel 'mid starry banners beam?
Quick throbs my breast at war's untried alarms,
Unknown pulsations stirr'd by glory's charms.

While dear Columbia calls, no danger awes,
Though certain death to threaten'd chains be join'd.
Though fails this flesh devote to freedom's cause,
Can death subdue th' unconquerable mind?
Or adamantine chains ethereal substance bind?

from The Address to the Armies of the United States of America

Hail, heaven-born Peace! thy grateful blessings pour
On this glad land, and round the peopled shore:
Thine are the joys that gild the happy scene,
Propitious days, and festive nights serene;
With thee gay Pleasure frolics o'er the plain,
And smiling Plenty leads thy prosperous train.

Then oh, my friends! the task of glory done,
Th' immortal prize by your bold efforts won;
Your country's saviours, by her voice confessed,
While unborn ages rise and call you blest;
Then let us go where happier climes invite,
To midland seas, and regions of delight;
With all that's ours, together let us rise,
Seek brighter plains and more indulgent skies;
Where fair Ohio rolls his amber tide,
And nature blossoms in her virgin pride;
Where all that beauty's hand can form to please,
Shall crown the toils of war with rural ease.

from The Hasty Pudding

Dear Hasty-Pudding, what unpromised joy
Expands my heart, to meet thee in Savoy!
Doom'd o'er the world through devious paths to roam,
Each clime my country, and each house my home,
My soul is soothed, my cares have found an end,
I greet my long-lost, unforgotten friend.

For thee through Paris, that corrupted town,
How long in vain I wandered up and down,
Where shameless Bacchus, with his drenching hoard,
Cold from his cave usurps the morning board.
London is lost in smoke and steep'd in tea;
No Yankee there can lisp the name of thee;
The uncouth word, a libel on the town,
Would call a proclamation from the crown.
From climes oblique, that fear the sun's full rays,
Chilled in their fogs, exclude the generous maize:
A grain whose rich, luxuriant growth requires
Short, gentle showers and bright, ethereal fires.

But here, though distant from our native shore,
With mutual glee we meet and laugh once more,
The same! I know thee by that yellow face,
That strong complexion of true Indian race,
Which time can never change, nor soil impair,
Nor Alpine snows, nor Turkey's morbid air;
For endless years, through every mild domain,
Where grows the maize, there thou art sure to reign.

But man, more fickle, the bold license claims,
In different realms to give thee different names.
Thee, the soft nations round the warm Levant
Polenta call, the French, of course, *Polente*.

E'en in thy native regions, how I blush
To hear the Pennsylvanians call thee *Mush*!
On Hudson's banks, while men of Belgic spawn
Insult and eat thee by the name Suppawn
All spurious appellations, void of truth;
I've better known thee from my earliest youth:
Thy name is *Hasty-Pudding*! thus my sire
Was wont to greet thee fuming from the fire;
And while he argued in thy just defence
With logic clear, he thus explained the sense:—
"In *haste* the boiling cauldron, o'er the blaze,
Receives and cooks the ready powdered maize;
In *haste* 'tis served, and then in equal *haste*,
With cooling milk, we make the sweet repast.
No carving to be done, no knife to grate
The tender ear, and wound the stony plate;
But the smooth spoon, just fitted to the lip,
And taught with art the yielding mass to dip,
By frequent journeys to the bowl well stored,
Performs the hasty honors of the board."
Such is thy name, significant and clear,
A name, a sound to every Yankee dear,
But most to me, whose heart and palate chaste
Preserve my pure hereditary taste.

There are who strive to stamp with disrepute
The luscious food, because it feeds the brute;
In tropes of high-strain'd wit, while gaudy prigs
Compare thy nursling man, to pamper'd pigs;
With sovereign scorn I treat the vulgar jest,
Nor fear to share thy bounties with the beast.
What though the generous cow gives me to quaff
The milk nutritious; am I then a calf?
Or can the genius of the noisy swine,
Though nursed on pudding, claim kin to mine?
Sure the sweet song, I fashion to thy praise,
Runs more melodious than the notes they raise.

My song resounding in its grateful glee,
No merit claims: I praise myself in thee.
My father loved thee through his length of days!
For thee his fields were shaded o'er with maize;
From thee what health, what vigor he possess'd,
Ten sturdy freemen from his loins attest;
Thy constellation ruled my natal morn,
And all my bones were made of Indian corn.
Delicious grain! whatever form it take,
To roast or boil, to smother or to bake,
In every dish 'tis welcome still to me,
But most, my *Hasty-Pudding*, most in thee.

Let the green succotash with thee contend,
Let beans and corn their sweetest juices blend,
Let butter drench them in its yellow tide,
And a long slice of bacon grace their side;
Not all the plate, how famed soe'er it be,
Can please my palate like a bowl of thee.

Some talk of Hoe-Cake, fair Virginia's pride,
Rich Johnny-Cake, this mouth has often tried;
Both please me well, their virtues much the same,
Alike their fabric, as allied their fame,
Except in dear New England, where the last
Receives a dash of pumpkin in the paste,
To give it sweetness and improve the taste.
But place them all before me, smoking hot,
The big, round dumpling, rolling from the pot,
The pudding of the bag, whose quivering breast,
With suet lined, leads on the Yankee feast,
The Charlotte brown, within whose crusty sides
A belly soft the pulpy apple hides;
The yellow bread whose face like amber glows,
And all the Indian that the bake-pan knows,—
Ye tempt me not, my fav'rite greets my eyes,
To that loved bowl my spoon by instinct flies.

from The Columbiad

To equal fame ascends thy tuneful throng,
The boast of genius and the pride of song;
Caught from the cast of every age and clime,
Their lays shall triumph o'er the lapse of time.

With lynx-eyed glance through nature far to pierce,
With all the powers and every charm of verse,
Each science opening in his ample mind,
His fancy glowing and his taste refined,
See TRUMBULL lead the train. His skillful hand
Hurls the keen darts of satire round the land.
Pride, knavery, dullness, feel his mortal stings,
And listening Virtue triumphs while he sings;
Britain's foiled sons, victorious now no more,
In guilt retiring from the wasted shore,
Strive their curst cruelties to hide in vain;
The world resounds them in his deathless strain.

On wings of faith to elevate the soul
Beyond the bourne of earth's benighted pole,
For DWIGHT's high harp the epic Muse sublime
Hails her new empire in the western clime.
Tuned from the tones by seers seraphic sung,
Heaven in his eye and rapture on his tongue,
His voice revives old Canaan's promised land,
The long-fought fields of JACOB's chosen band.
In HANNIEL's fate proud faction finds its doom,
Ai's midnight flames light nations to their tomb;
In visions bright supernal joys are given,
And all the dark futurities of heaven.

While Freedom's cause his patriot bosom warms,
In counsel sage, nor inexpert in arms,
See HUMPHREYS glorious from the field retire,
Sheathe the glad sword and string the soothing lyre;
That lyre which erst, in hours of dark despair,
Roused the sad realms to finish well the war.
O'er fallen friends, with all the strength of woe,
Fraternal sighs in his strong numbers flow;
His country's wrongs, her duties, dangers, praise,
Fire his full soul and animate his lays:
Wisdom and war with equal joy shall own
So fond a votary and so brave a son.

from The Judgment, A Vision

IV.

Then on the mount, amidst these glorious shapes,
Who reverent stood, with looks of sacred awe,
I saw EMMANUEL seated on his throne.
His robe, methought, was whiter than the light;
Upon his breast the Heavenly Urim glowed
Bright as the sun, and round such lightnings flashed,
No eye could meet the mystic symbol's blaze.
Irradiant the eternal sceptre shone
Which wont to glitter in his Father's hand:
Resplendent in his face the Godhead beamed,
Justice and mercy, majesty and grace,
Divinely mingling. Celestial glories played
Around with beamy lustre; from his eye
Dominion looked; upon his brow was stamped
Creative Power. Yet, over all the touch
Of gracious pity dwelt, which, erst, amidst
Dissolving nature's anguish breathed a prayer
For guilty man. Redundant down his neck
His locks rolled graceful, as they waved, of old,
Upon the mournful breeze of Calvary.

. . . .

XVIII.

Sage faces, grave and firm, with war-worn locks,
Around a venerable Sire I saw,
Whose hoary head, with patriot glory crown'd,
Eclipsed the lustre of the diadem.
On their bold brows appeared that settled soul
Racks cannot shake, nor fiercest thunderbolts,
By Tyrants fulmined; not for gold, nor spoil
Torn from an injured people, not to gloss
Some Monarch's purple with a bloodier die,
Their swords were sheathless: in the sacred cause
Of man's essential, inborn liberties,
Inherent, deathless as his soul, they drew.
They were the Watchmen by an Empire's cradle
Whose youthful sinews show like Rome's; whose head
Tempestuous rears with ice-encrusted cap
Sparkling with Polar splendours, while her skirts
Catch perfumes from the Isles; whose trident, yet,
Must awe in either ocean; whose strong hand
Freedom's immortal banner grasps, and waves
Its spangled glories o'er the envying world.

. . . .

XXIII.

Low warblings, now, and solitary harps
Were heard among the Angels, touched and tuned
As to an evening hymn, preluding soft
To Cherub voices; louder as they swelled
Deep strings struck in, and hoarser instruments,
Mixed with clear silver sounds, till concord rose
Full as the harmony of winds to heaven;
Yet sweet as nature's springtide melodies
To some worn Pilgrim first with glistening eyes
Greeting his native valley, whence the sounds
Of rural gladness, herds, and bleating flocks,
The chirp of birds, blithe voices, lowing kine,
The dash of waters, reed, or rustic pipe,
Blent with the dulcet distance-mellowed bell,
Come, like the echo of his early joys.
In every pause, from spirits in mid air,
Responsive still were golden viols heard,
And Heavenly symphonies stole faintly down.

from Sachem's Wood

Seldom, a real scene you see
So full of sweet variety;
The distant, flowing, bold, and grand.
I've seen the world, from side to side,
Walked in the ways of human pride,
Mused in palaces of kings,
And know what wealth to grandeur brings;
The spot for *me*, of all the earth,
Is this, the dear one of my birth.
Go, search the page of Grecian lore,
Scan all the men, and deeds, of yore,
Read *how* the Kingless Power grew great,
And note how wolf-cubs found a state;
Go, quaff with robbers in their cave;
Try, what distinction reason's eye,
Twixt towers and caverns can espy.
Then mark how our "Seven Pillars" rise,
Built up, like those which prop the skies,
On Justice, Truth, and Peace and Love,
With Grace cemented from Above!
Where is the violence or wrong,
Done to the weak, as we grew strong?
Where is the record of disgrace
We blush, or ought to blush, to face?
What landless Indian could declare
Our shameful arts to peel him bare?
Or, justly change, if armed with powers,
A mete or landmark claimed as ours?
The spot most *blameless* of the earth
Is this, the sweet one of my birth;
This, and the land where virtuous Pen
Followed his Saviour out, with men.

The Western Emigrant

An axe rang sharply mid those forest shades
Which from creation toward the skies had towered
In unshorn beauty. There, with vigorous arm
Wrought a bold Emigrant, and by his side
His little son, with question and response,
Beguiled the toil.
"Boy, thou hast never seen
Such glorious trees. Hark, when their giant trunks
Fall, how the firm earth groans! Rememberest thou
The mighty river, on whose breast we sailed,
So many days, on toward the setting sun?
Our own Connecticut, compared to that,
Was but a creeping stream."
"Father, the brook
That by our door went singing, where I launched
My tiny boat, with my young playmates round,
When school was o'er, is dearer far to me,
Than all these bold, broad waters. To my eye
They are as strangers. And those little trees
My mother nurtured in the garden bound,
Of our first home, from whence the fragrant peach
Hung in its ripening gold, were fairer, sure,
Than this dark forest, shutting out the day."
—"What ho!—my little girl!" and with light step
A fairy creature hasted toward her sire,
And, setting down the basket that contained
His noon's repast, looked upward to his face
With sweet confiding smile.
"See, dearest, see,
That bright-winged paroquet, and hear the song
Of yon gay red-bird, echoing through the trees,
Making rich music. Didst thou ever hear,
In far New England, such a mellow tone?"
—"I had a robin that did take the crumbs

Each night and morning, and his chirping voice
Did make me joyful, as I went to tend
My snow-drops. I was always laughing then
In that first home. I should be happier now
Methinks, if I could find among these dells
The same fresh violets."
Slow night drew on,
And round the rude hut of the Emigrant
The wrathful spirit of the rising storm
Spake bitter things. His weary children slept,
And he, with head declined, sat listening long
To the swoln waters of the Illinois,
Dashing against their shores.
Starting he spake—
"Wife! did I see thee brush away a tear?
'Twas even so. Thy heart was with the halls
Of thy nativity. Their sparkling lights,
Carpets, and sofas, and admiring guests,
Befit thee better than these rugged walls
Of shapeless logs, and this lone, hermit-home."
"No—no. All was so still around, methought
Upon mine ear that echoed hymn did steal,
Which mid the church, where erst we paid our vows,
So tuneful pealed. But tenderly thy voice
Dissolved the illusion." And the gentle smile
Lighting her brow, the fond caress that soothed
Her waking infant, re-assured his soul
That, wheresoe'er our best affections dwell
And strike a healthful root, is happiness.
Content, and placid, to his rest he sank;
But dreams, those wild magicians, that do play
Such pranks when reason slumbers, tireless wrought
Their will with him.
Up rose the thronging mart
Of his own native city—roof and spire,
All glittering bright, in fancy's frost-work ray.
The steed his boyhood nurtured proudly neighed,
The favorite dog came frisking round his feet,
With shrill and joyous bark—familiar doors
Flew open—greeting hands with his were linked
In friendship's grasp—he heard the keen debate
From congregated haunts, where mind with mind
Doth blend and brighten—and till morning roved
Mid the loved scenery of his native land.

Death of an Infant

Death found strange beauty on that polished brow,
And dashed it out. There was a tint of rose
On cheek and lip. He touched the veins with ice,
And the rose faded.
                                        Forth from those blue eyes
There spake a wishful tenderness, a doubt
Whether to grieve or sleep, which innocence
Alone may wear. With ruthless haste he bound
The silken fringes of those curtaining lids
For ever.
                    There had been a murmuring sound,
With which the babe would claim its mother's ear,
Charming her even to tears. The spoiler set
The seal of silence.
                                        But there beamed a smile,
So fixed, so holy, from that cherub brow,
Death gazed, and left it there. He dared not steal
The signet-ring of heaven!

The War-Spirit

WAR-SPIRIT! War-Spirit! how gorgeous thy path,
Pale Earth shrinks with fear from thy chariot of wrath,
The king at thy beckoning comes down from his throne,
To the conflict of fate the armed nations rush on,
With the trampling of steeds, and the trumpet's wild cry,
While the folds of their banners gleam bright o'er the sky.

Thy glories are sought, till the life-throb is o'er,
Thy laurels pursued, though they blossom in gore,
Mid the ruins of columns and temples sublime,
The arch of the hero doth grapple with time;
The Muse o'er thy form throws her tissue divine,
And History her annal emblazons with thine.

War-Spirit! War-Spirit! thy secrets are known,
I have looked on the field when the battle was done,
The mangled and slain in their misery lay,
And the vulture was shrieking and watching his prey;
But the heart's gush of sorrow, how hopeless and sore,
In the homes that those loved ones revisit no more.

I have traced out thy march, by its features of pain,
While Famine and Pestilence stalked in thy train,
And the trophies of sin did thy victory swell,
And thy breath on the soul, was the plague-spot of hell;
Death lauded thy deeds, and in letters of flame
The realm of perdition recorded thy name.

War-Spirit! War-Spirit! go down to thy place,
With the demons that thrive on the woe of our race;
Call back thy strong legions of madness and pride,
Bid the rivers of blood thou hast opened be dried—
Let thy league with the grave and Aceldama cease,
And yield the torn world to the Angel of Peace.

Indian Names

"How can the red men be forgotten, while so many of our states and territories, bays, lakes and rivers, are indelibly stamped by names of their giving?"

Ye say they all have passed away,
That noble race and brave,
That their light canoes have vanished
From off the crested wave;
That 'mid the forests where they roamed
There rings no hunter shout,
But their name is on your waters,
Ye may not wash it out.

'Tis where Ontario's billow
Like Ocean's surge is curled,
Where strong Niagara's thunders wake
The echo of the world.
Where red Missouri bringeth
Rich tribute from the west,
And Rappahannock sweetly sleeps
On green Virginia's breast.

Ye say their cone-like cabins,
That clustered o'er the vale,
Have fled away like withered leaves
Before the autumn gale,
But their memory liveth on your hills,
Their baptism on your shore,
Your everlasting rivers speak
Their dialect of yore.

Old Massachusetts wears it,
Within her lordly crown,
And broad Ohio bears it,
Amid his young renown;
Connecticut hath wreathed it
Where her quiet foliage waves,
And bold Kentucky breathed it hoarse
Through all her ancient caves.

Wachuset hides its lingering voice
  Within his rocky heart,
And Alleghany graves its tone
  Throughout his lofty chart;
Monadnock on his forehead hoar
  Doth seal the sacred trust,
Your mountains build their monument,
  Though ye destroy their dust.

Ye call these red-browed brethren
  The insects of an hour,
Crushed like the noteless worm amid
  The regions of their power;
Ye drive them from their father's lands,
  Ye break of faith the seal,
But can ye from the court of Heaven
  Exclude their last appeal?

Ye see their unresisting tribes,
  With toilsome step and slow,
On through the trackless desert pass,
  A caravan of woe;
Think ye the Eternal's ear is deaf?
  His sleepless vision dim?
Think ye the *soul's blood* may not cry
  From that far land to him?

The Old Psalm Tune

You asked, dear friend, the other day,
  Why still my charmèd ear
Rejoiceth in uncultured tone
  That old psalm tune to hear?

I've heard full oft, in foreign lands,
  The grand orchestral strain,
Where music's ancient masters live,
  Revealed on earth again,—

Where breathing, solemn instruments,
  In swaying clouds of sound,
Bore up the yearning, trancèd soul,
  Like silver wings around;—

I've heard in old St. Peter's dome,
  Where clouds of incense rise,
Most ravishing the choral swell
  Mount upwards to the skies.

And well I feel the magic power,
  When skilled and cultured art
Its cunning webs of sweetness weaves
  Around the captured heart.

But yet, dear friend, though rudely sung,
  That old psalm tune hath still
A pulse of power beyond them all
  My inmost soul to thrill.

Those halting tones that sound to you,
  Are not the tones I hear;
But voices of the loved and lost
  There meet my longing ear.

I hear my angel mother's voice,—
  Those were the words she sung;
I hear my brother's ringing tones,
  As once on earth they rung;

And friends that walk in white above
  Come round me like a cloud,
And far above those earthly notes
  Their singing sounds aloud.

There may be discord, as you say;
  Those voices poorly ring;
But there's no discord in the strain
  Those upper spirits sing.

For they who sing are of the blest,
  The calm and glorified,
Whose hours are one eternal rest
  On heaven's sweet floating tide.

Their life is music and accord;
  Their souls and hearts keep time
In one sweet concert with the Lord,—
  One concert vast, sublime.

And through the hymns they sang on earth
  Sometimes a sweetness falls
On those they loved and left below,
  And softly homeward calls,—

Bells from our own dear fatherland,
  Borne trembling o'er the sea,—
The narrow sea that they have crossed,
  The shores where we shall be.

O sing, sing on, belovèd souls!
  Sing cares and griefs to rest;
Sing, till entrancèd we arise
  To join you 'mong the blest

Above

A VISION

Coming down a golden street
I beheld my vanished one,
And he moveth on a cloud,
And his forehead wears a star;
And his blue eyes, deep and holy,
Fixed as in a blessed dream,
See some mystery of joy,
Some unuttered depth of love.

And his vesture is as blue
As the skies of summer are,
Falling with a saintly sweep,
With a sacred stillness swaying;
And he presseth to his bosom
Harp of strange and mystic fashion,
And his hands, like living pearls,
Wander o'er the golden strings.

And the music that ariseth,
Who can utter or divine it?
In that strange celestial thrilling,
Every memory of sorrow,
Every heart-ache, every anguish,
Every fear for the to-morrow,
Melt away in charmèd rest.

And there be around him many,
Bright with robes like evening clouds,—
Tender green and clearest amber,
Crimson fading into rose,
Robes of flames and robes of silver,—
And their hues all thrill and tremble
With a living light of feeling,
Deepening with each heart's pulsation,
Till in vivid trance of color
That celestial rainbow glows.

How they float and wreathe and brighten,
Bending low their starry brows,
Singing with a tender cadence,
And their hands, like spotless lilies,
Folded on their prayerful breasts.
In their singing seem to mingle
Tender airs of by-gone days;—
Mother-hymnings by the cradle,
Mother-moanings by the grave,
Songs of human love and sorrow,
Songs of endless love and rest;—
In the pauses of that music
Every throb of sorrow dies.

O my own, my heart's belovèd,
Vainly have I wept above thee?
Would I call thee from thy glory
To this world's impurity?—
Lo! it passeth, it dissolveth,
All the vision melts away;
But as if a heavenly lily
Dropped into my aching breast,
With a healing sweetness laden,
With a mystic breath of rest,
I am charmed into forgetting
Autumn winds and dreary grave.

The Miserere

Not of the earth that music! all things fade;
Vanish the pictured walls! and, one by one,
The starry candles silently expire!

And now, O Jesus! round that silent cross
A moment's pause, a hush as of the grave.
Now rises slow a silver mist of sound,
And all the heavens break out in drops of grief;
A rain of sobbing sweetness, swelling, dying,
Voice into voice inweaving with sweet throbs,
And fluttering pulses of impassioned moan,—
Veiled voices, in whose wailing there is awe,
And mysteries of love and agony,
A yearning anguish of celestial souls,
A shiver as of wings trembling the air,
As if God's shining doves, his spotless birds,
Wailed with a nightingale's heart-break of grief,
In this their starless night, when for our sins
Their sun, their life, their love, hangs darkly there,
Like a slain lamb, bleeding his life away!

Suspiria Ensis

Mourn no more for our dead,
Laid in their rest serene—
With tears a Land hath shed
Their graves shall ever be green.

Ever their fair, true glory
Fondly shall fame rehearse—
Light of legend and story,
Flower of marble and verse!

(Wilt thou forget, O Mother!
How thy darlings, day by day,
For thee, and with fearless faces,
Journeyed the darksome way—
Went down to death in the war-ship,
And on the bare hill-side lay?)

For the Giver they gave their breath,
And 'tis now no time to mourn—
Lo, of their dear, brave death
A mighty Nation is born!

But a long lament for others,
Dying for Darker Powers!—
Those that once were our brothers,
Whose children shall yet be ours.

That a People, haughty and brave,
(Warriors, old and young!)
Should lie in a bloody grave,
And never a dirge be sung!

We may look with woe on the dead,
We may smooth their lids, 'tis true,
For the veins of a common red
And the Mother's milk we drew.

But alas, how vainly bleeds
The breast that is bared for Crime—
Who shall dare hymn the deeds
That else had been all sublime?

Were it alien steel that clashed,
They had guarded each inch of sod—
But the angry valor dashed
On the awful shield of God!

(Ah—if for some great Good—
On some giant Evil hurled—
The Thirty Millions had stood
'Gainst the might of a banded world!)

But now, to the long, long Night
They pass, as they ne'er had been—
A stranger and sadder sight
Than ever the sun hath seen.

For his waning beams illume
A vast and a sullen train
Going down to the gloom—
One wretched and drear refrain
The only line on their tomb,—
"They died—and they died in vain!"

Gone—ay me!—to the grave,
And never one note of song—
The Muse would weep for the brave,
But how shall she chant the wrong?

For a wayward Wench is she—
One that rather would wait
With Old John Brown at the tree
Than Stonewall dying in state.

When, for the wrongs that were,
  Hath she lilted a single stave?
Know, proud hearts, that, with her,
  'Tis not enough to be brave.

By the injured, with loving glance,
  Aye hath she lingered of old,
And eyed the Evil askance,
  Be it never so haught and bold.

With Homer, alms-gift in hand,
  With Dante, exile and free,
With Milton, blind in the Strand,
  With Hugo, lone by the sea!

In the attic, with Berangér,
  She could carol, how blithe and free!
Of the old, worn Frocks of Blue,
  (All threadbare with victory!)
But never of purple and gold,
  Never of Lily or Bee!

And thus, though the Traitor Sword
  Were the bravest that battle wields—
Though the fiery Valor poured
  Its life on a thousand fields—

The sheen of its ill renown
  All tarnished with guilt and blame,
No Poet a deed may crown,
  No Lay may laurel a name.

Yet never for thee, fair Song!
  The fallen brave to condemn;
They died for a mighty Wrong—
  But their Demon died with them.

(Died, by field and by city!)—
  Be thine on the day to dwell,
When dews of peace and of pity
  Shall fall o'er the fading hell—

And the dead shall smile in Heaven—
  And tears, that now may not rise,
Of love and of all forgiveness,
  Shall stream from a million eyes.

Flag Ship Hartford, at Sea,
January, 1864

A War Study

Methinks, all idly and too well
  We love this Nature—little care
  (Whate'er her children brave and bear,)
Were hers, though any grief befell.

With gayer sunshine still she seeks
  To gild our trouble, so 'twould seem;
  Through all this long, tremendous Dream,
A tear hath never wet her cheeks.

And such a scene I call to mind—
  The third day's thunder, (fort and fleet,
  And the great guns beneath our feet,)
Was dying, and a warm gulf wind

Made monotone 'mid stays and shrouds:
  O'er books and men in quiet chat
  With the Great Admiral I sat,
Watching the lovely cannon-clouds.

For still, from mortar and from gun,
  Or short-fused shell that burst aloft,
  Outsprung a rose-wreath, bright and soft,
Tinged with the redly setting sun.

And I their beauty praised: but he,
  The grand old Senior, strong and mild,
  (Of head a sage, in heart a child,)
Sighed for the wreck that still must be.

Flag Ship Hartford,
March, 1864

All Together

Old friends and dear! it were ungentle rhyme,
  If I should question of your true hearts, whether
Ye have forgotten that far, pleasant time,
  The good old time when we were all together.

Our limbs were lusty and our souls sublime;
  We never heeded cold and winter weather,
Nor sun nor travel, in that cheery time,
  The brave old time when we were all together.

Pleasant it was to tread the mountain thyme,
  Sweet was the pure and piny mountain ether,
And pleasant all; but this was in the time,
  The good old time when we were all together.

Since then I've strayed through many a fitful clime,
  (Tossed on the wind of fortune like a feather,)
And chanced with rare good fellows in my time—
  Bur ne'er the time that we have known together:

But none like those brave hearts, (for now I climb
  Gray hills alone, or thread the lonely heather,)
That walked beside me in the ancient time,
  The good old time when we were all together.

Long since, we parted in our careless prime,
  Like summer birds no June shall hasten hither;
No more to meet as in that merry time,
  The sweet spring-time that shone on all together.

Some, to the fevered city's toil and grime,
  And some o'er distant seas, and some—ah! whither?
Nay, we shall never meet as in the time,
  The dear old time when we were all together.

And some—above their heads, in wind and rime,
  Year after year, the grasses wave and wither;
Ayc, wc shall meet!—'tis but a little time,
  And all shall lie with folded hands together.

And if, beyond the sphere of doubt and crime,
   Lie purer lands—ah! let our steps be thither;
That, done with earthly change and earthly time,
   In God's good time we may be all together.

In Duty Bound

In duty bound, a life hemmed in
  Whichever way the spirit turns to look;
No chance of breaking out, except by sin;
    Not even room to shirk—
    Simply to live, and work.

An obligation pre-imposed, unsought,
  Yet binding with the force of natural law;
The pressure of antagonistic thought;
    Aching within, each hour,
    A sense of wasting power.

A house with roof so darkly low
  The heavy rafters shut the sunlight out;
One cannot stand erect without a blow;
    Until the soul inside
    Cries for a grave—more wide.

A consciousness that if this thing endure,
  The common joys of life will dull the pain;
The high ideals of the grand and pure
    Die, as of course they must,
    Of long disuse and rust.

That is the worst. It takes supernal strength
  To hold the attitude that brings the pain;
And they are few indeed but stoop at length
    To something less than best,
    To find, in stooping, rest.

To the Young Wife

Are you content, you pretty three-years' wife?
  Are you content and satisfied to live
  On what your loving husband loves to give,
    And give him your life?

Are you content with work,—to toil alone,
  To clean things dirty and to soil things clean;
  To be a kitchen-maid, be called a queen,—
    Queen of a cook-stove throne?

Are you content to reign in that small space—
  A wooden palace and a yard-fenced land—
  With other queens abundant on each hand,
    Each fastened in her place?

Are you content to rear your children so?
  Untaught yourself, untrained, perplexed, distressed,
  Are you so sure your way is always best?
    That you can always know?

Have you forgotten how you used to long
  In days of ardent girlhood, to be great,
  To help the groaning world, to serve the state,
    To be so wise—so strong?

And are you quite convinced this is the way,
  The only way a woman's duty lies—
  Knowing all women so have shut their eyes?
    Seeing the world to-day?

Have you no dream of life in fuller store?
  Of growing to be more than that you are?
  Doing the things you now do better far,
    Yet doing others—more?

Losing no love, but finding as you grew
  That as you entered upon nobler life
  You so became a richer, sweeter wife,
    A wiser mother too?

What holds you? Ah, my dear, it is your throne,
  Your paltry queenship in that narrow place,
  Your antique labors, your restricted space,
    Your working all alone!

Be not deceived! 'Tis not your wifely bond
  That holds you, nor the mother's royal power,
  But selfish, slavish service hour by hour—
    A life with no beyond!

Connecticut Road Song

In the wide and rocky pasture where the cedar
trees are gray,
The briar rose was growing with the blueberry and
bay.
The girls went forth to pick them and the lads
went out to play,
But I had to get to Stonington before the break of
day.

And when I came to Stonington, she was a town
of pride.
"Come in," they said, "and labor, and be at home
and bide.
For gold shall be thy wage," but 'twas past the hour
of morn—
And I had to get to Jordan while the dew was on
the thorn.

There is a girl at Jordan, she sweetly smiled at me,
As pale as are the berries on the gray cedar tree.
And "Oh," she cried, "thou traveler, come bide
awhile with me,"
But I had to get to Lebanon while light was in the
tree.

The pale church spires of Lebanon shone sweet
upon the sky.
The Sabbath bells were ringing, the parson passed
me by.
"Oh wait, traveler, wait, for you've need to say a
prayer,"
But I had to be in Wallingford while noon was in
the air.

The road that leads to Wallingford, it runs through mire and stone.
I was parched with the dust, I was bleeding and alone.
"My lad, you will die, if you do not tarry here."
But I had to get to Killingworth while day was on the mere.

And when I got to Killingworth I heard the people say
"He has come to bring the news from a hundred miles away."
But I had not any news and not any time to stay,
For I had to be at Jericho before the end of day.

And when I came to Jericho I heard the people call,
"Do you run to save a city that you will not wait at all?"
"I run to save no city, yet must I leave you soon,
For I have to be in Windsor with the rising of the moon."

And when I got to Windsor, then was I spent for bread.
"Come in," they cried, "poor traveler! and be thou comforted.
What strange great need is on thee that makes thee journey so?"
But I had to be in Coventry ere yet the moon was low.

For a strange great need was on me that I should hunt the rain,
And take into my body a breakage and a pain;
That I should tame the sunset and goad the hurrying plain,
And that the leagues behind me should lie a thousand slain.

Wherefore, ye men of Coventry, if ye desire to stay,
Lay not your curb upon me, that love the open way.
For I want to smell the dew, the blueberry and the bay,
And I have to get to Colchester before the break of day.

Inheritance

They left to me their house and lands
Who am next of kin.
On what was theirs I lay my hands
And freely I go in.

Before the hearth where they once sat
I speak my yes and no.
I am the master over it
Who once would come and go.

I would repeat the bitter sting
Of all my early need,
Yes, I would own not anything
But have them here indeed.

I would resign my years of right
If I could hear them say;
"We cannot let you go to-night"
Or, "Come and spend the day."

Now this estate lies broad and fair
As far as eye can see.
But not a voice breaks on the air
And no one speaks to me.

First Letter

I have a beautiful home on the slope of a green, green hillside.
Sometimes it shines so bright, it seems like silver to me.
There are roses, lovely and tall, and the song birds sing all around it.
And there is a view below that looks off over the sea.

Yes, we have things to eat, but they are not such as you have—
Bacon and pancakes and pudding, coffee and sausage and pie—
But a bread that comforts the soul sweeter than apples or honey;
Fresher than lilies or roses is the food we are nourished by.

Richard is here and he goes off to the College each day
With glorious books.
He is happy and friendly and has funny things to say,
And buoyant and gay in his looks.

If you could only see me now in my beautiful golden chamber,
Free to come and to go,
Free and happy and well—free—unutterably free.

I wish you could see the flowers and hear the birds we have here.
Silence . . . Sometimes I am with people;
Sometimes I have things to do . . . infinite leisure.
Sometimes music is here and color and shape and happy talk . . .

Water . . . but not with a rush and a roar.
But it seemed a quiet pool filled with exquisite lilies.
Only have courage and know there is nothing to fear.

When I went that night my manner of going seemed easy.
I sat up in my bed and put my feet on the floor.
Then I went out and away but not through the door nor the window.
I went by a secret path, a narrow invisible door.

Thirteen Ways of Looking at a Blackbird

I

Among twenty snowy mountains,
The only moving thing
Was the eye of the blackbird.

II

I was of three minds,
Like a tree
In which there are three blackbirds.

III

The blackbird whirled in the autumn winds.
It was a small part of the pantomime.

IV

A man and a woman
Are one.
A man and a woman and a blackbird
Are one.

V

I do not know which to prefer,
The beauty of inflections
Or the beauty of innuendoes,
The blackbird whistling
Or just after.

VI

Icicles filled the long window
With barbaric glass.
The shadow of the blackbird
Crossed it, to and fro.
The mood
Traced in the shadow
An indecipherable cause.

VII

O thin men of Haddam,
Why do you imagine golden birds?
Do you not see how the blackbird
Walks around the feet
Of the women about you?

VIII

I know noble accents
And lucid, inescapable rhythms;
But I know, too,
That the blackbird is involved
In what I know.

IX

When the blackbird flew out of sight,
It marked the edge
Of one of many circles.

X

At the sight of blackbirds
Flying in a green light,
Even the bawds of euphony
Would cry out sharply.

XI

He rode over Connecticut
In a glass coach.
Once, a fear pierced him,
In that he mistook
The shadow of his equipage
For blackbirds.

XII

The river is moving.
The blackbird must be flying.

XIII

It was evening all afternoon.
It was snowing
And it was going to snow.
The blackbird sat
In the cedar-limbs.

Of Hartford in a Purple Light

A long time you have been making the trip
From Havre to Hartford, Master Soleil,
Bringing the lights of Norway and all that.

A long time the ocean has come with you,
Shaking the water off, like a poodle,
That splatters incessant thousands of drops,

Each drop a petty tricolor. For this,
The aunts in Pasadena, remembering,
Abhor the plaster of the western horses,

Souvenirs of museums. But, Master, there are
Lights masculine and lights feminine.
What is this purple, this parasol,

This stage-light of the Opera?
It is like a region full of intonings.
It is Hartford seen in a purple light.

A moment ago, light masculine,
Working, with big hands, on the town,
Arranged its heroic attitudes.

But now as in an amour of women
Purple sets purple round. Look, Master,
See the river, the railroad, the cathedral . . .

When male light fell on the naked back
Of the town, the river, the railroad were clear.
Now, every muscle slops away.

Hi! Whisk it, poodle, flick the spray
Of the ocean, ever-freshening,
On the irised hunks, the stone bouquet.

from An Ordinary Evening in New Haven

I

The eye's plain version is a thing apart,
The vulgate of experience. Of this,
A few words, an and yet, and yet, and yet—

As part of the never-ending meditation,
Part of the question that is a giant himself:
Of what is this house composed if not of the sun,

These houses, these difficult objects, dilapidate
Appearances of what appearances,
Words, lines, not meanings, not communications,

Dark things without a double, after all,
Unless a second giant kills the first—
A recent imagining of reality,

Much like a new resemblance of the sun,
Down-pouring, up-springing and inevitable,
A larger poem for a larger audience,

As if the crude collops came together as one,
A mythological form, a festival sphere,
A great bosom, beard and being, alive with age.

II

Suppose these houses are composed of ourselves,
So that they become an impalpable town, full of
Impalpable bells, transparencies of sound,

Sounding in transparent dwellings of the self,
Impalpable habitations that seem to move
In the movement of the colors of the mind,

The far-fire flowing and the dim-coned bells
Coming together in a sense in which we are poised,
Without regard to time or where we are,

In the perpetual reference, object
Of the perpetual meditation, point
Of the enduring, visionary love,

Obscure, in colors whether of the sun
Or mind, uncertain in the clearest bells,
The spirit's speeches, the indefinite,

Confused illuminations and sonorities,
So much ourselves, we cannot tell apart
The idea and the bearer-being of the idea.

III

The point of vision and desire are the same.
It is to the hero of midnight that we pray
On a hill of stones to make beau mont thereof.

If it is misery that infuriates our love,
If the black of night stands glistening on beau
mont,
Then, ancientest saint ablaze with ancientest truth,

Say next to holiness is the will thereto,
And next to love is the desire for love,
The desire for its celestial ease in the heart,

Which nothing can frustrate, that most secure,
Unlike love in possession of that which was
To be possessed and is. But this cannot

Possess. It is desire, set deep in the eye,
Behind all actual seeing, in the actual scene,
In the street, in a room, on a carpet or a wall,

Always in emptiness that would be filled,
In denial that cannot contain its blood,
A porcelain, as yet in the bats thereof.

IV

The plainness of plain things is savagery,
As: the last plainness of a man who has fought
Against illusion and was, in a great grinding

Of growling teeth, and falls at night, snuffed out
By the obese opiates of sleep. Plain men in plain
towns
Are not precise about the appeasement they need.

They only know a savage assuagement cries
With a savage voice; and in that cry they hear
Themselves transposed, muted and comforted

In a savage and subtle and simple harmony,
A matching and mating of surprised accords,
A responding to a diviner opposite.

So lewd spring comes from winter's chastity.
So, after summer, in the autumn air,
Comes the cold volume of forgotten ghosts,

But soothingly, with pleasant instruments,
So that this cold, a children's tale of ice,
Seems like a sheen of heat romanticized.

V

Inescapable romance, inescapable choice
Of dreams, disillusion as the last illusion,
Reality as a thing seen by the mind,

Not that which is but that which is apprehended,
A mirror, a lake of reflections in a room,
A glassy ocean lying at the door,

A great town hanging pendent in a shade,
An enormous nation happy in a style,
Everything as unreal as real can be,

In the inexquisite eye. Why, then, inquire
Who has divided the world, what entrepreneur?
No man. The self, the chrysalis of all men

Became divided in the leisure of blue day
And more, in branchings after day. One part
Held fast tenaciously in common earth

And one from central earth to central sky
And in moonlit extensions of them in the mind
Searched out such majesty as it could find.

The Plain Sense of Things

After the leaves have fallen, we return
To a plain sense of things. It is as if
We had come to an end of the imagination,
Inanimate in an inert savoir.

It is difficult even to choose the adjective
For this blank cold, this sadness without cause.
The great structure has become a minor house.
No turban walks across the lessened floors.

The greenhouse never so badly needed paint.
The chimney is fifty years old and slants to one side.
A fantastic effort has failed, a repetition
In a repetitiousness of men and flies.

Yet the absence of the imagination had
Itself to be imagined. The great pond,
The plain sense of it, without reflections, leaves,
Mud, water like dirty glass, expressing silence

Of a sort, silence of a rat come out to see,
The great pond and its waste of the lilies, all this
Had to be imagined as an inevitable knowledge,
Required, as a necessity requires.

The River of Rivers in Connecticut

There is a great river this side of Stygia,
Before one comes to the first black cataracts
And trees that lack the intelligence of trees.

In that river, far this side of Stygia,
The mere flowing of the water is a gayety,
Flashing and flashing in the sun. On its banks,

No shadow walks. The river is fateful,
Like the last one. But there is no ferryman.
He could not bend against its propelling force.

It is not to be seen beneath the appearances
That tell of it. The steeple at Farmington
Stands glistening and Haddam shines and sways.

It is the third commonness with light and air,
A curriculum, a vigor, a local abstraction . . .
Call it, once more, a river, an unnamed flowing,

Space-filled, reflecting the seasons, the folk-lore
Of each of the senses; call it, again and again,
The river that flows nowhere, like a sea.

Going Home

His thought of it was like a button pressed.
Far away the figures started going;
A silver watch ticked in a sleepy vest,
And on the porch an apron string was blowing.

His thought again was like a fly-wheel cranked,
And circular machinery set gliding.
The little town turned truly, as the banked
Brown houses followed in and out of hiding.

His travel, once he went, was like the troop
Of farmers in an autumn to the fair.
All year the field was flat, but now the coop
Of turkeys and the horses would be there;

People moving everywhere and nodding,
Little boys with birds and yellow whips;
A person at a counter would be wadding
Rifles, and the girls would hold their hips.

His coming near was like the soft arrival
Of gods around a thing that they have made;
And will again forget; but long survival
Saves it, once again the trance is laid.

The Unknown Army

We are the civil fathers, the poor necessary
Clerks of a fair world great death besieges.
Close and far the danger; ships and houses
Equally expect ambush; the foe's line
Is not one thread, is fabric: a cold cap
That tightens. And the young ones have departed.
In companies destructive, daring fate
To find them, they are deepest in the net
To rend it; and they will, and the free skull,
Warm again, should praise their blood forever.
We have not gone, nor may we; except darkly
In dreams—oh, then we bitterly deploy,
We venture; and arrive at the most difficult
Crossways, where the frost is quickest formed
On heroes. Which anonymous we are,
In nightmares—oh, the cursing in those thickets
When with no moon we come; only with heated
Hatred, searching midnight for a nerve
To sever in the arm that weaves this skeleton
Cloth, this whited silence, this green country's
Shroud that in our sleep we shear away.

The Seven Sleepers

The liberal arts lie eastward of this shore.
Choppy the waves at first. Then the long swells
And the being lost. Oh, centuries of salt
Till the surf booms again, and comes more land.

Not even there, except that old men point
At passes up the mountains. Over which,
Oh, centuries of soil, with olive trees
For twisted shade, and helicons for sound.

Then eastward seas, boned with peninsulas.
Then, orient, the islands; and at last,
The cave, the seven sleepers. Who will rise
And sing to you in numbers till you know

White magic. Which remember. Do you hear?
Oh, universe of sand that you must cross,
And animal the night. But do not rest.
The centuries are stars, and stud the way.

Anger in the Room

The hills of little Cornwall
Themselves are dreams.
The mind lies down among them,
Even by day, and snores,
Snug in the perilous knowledge
That nothing more inward pleasing,
More like itself,
Sleeps anywhere beyond them
Even by night
In the great land it cares two pins about,
Possibly; not more.

The mind, eager for caresses,
Lies down at its own risk in Cornwall;
Whose hills,
Whose cunning streams,
Whose mazes where a thought,
Doubling upon itself,
Considers the way, lazily, well lost,
Indulge it to the nick of death—
Not quite, for where it curls it still can feel,
Like feathers,
Like affectionate mouse whiskers,
The flattery, the trap.

Small White House

The sun of July beats down on the small white house.
The pasture is brown-bright as brass, and like brass, sings with heat.
Halt! And I stand here, hills shudder, withdraw into distance,
Leprous with light. And a child's cry comes from the house.

Tell me, oh, where, in what state, did I see the small white house,
Which I see in my mind?—And the wax-wing's beak slices the blue cedar-berry,
Which is as blue as distance. The river, far off, shrinks
Among the hot boulders, no glister, looks dead as a discarded snake-skin
rubbed off on stone. The house

Swims in that dazzle of no-Time. The child's cry comes from the house.

Evening Hawk

From plane of light to plane, wings dipping through
Geometries and orchids that the sunset builds,
Out of the peak's black angularity of shadow, riding
The last tumultuous avalanche of
Light above pines and the guttural gorge,
The hawk comes.

                    His wing
Scythes down another day, his motion
Is that of the honed steel-edge, we hear
The crashless fall of stalks of Time.

The head of each stalk is heavy with the gold of our error.

Look! look! he is climbing the last light
Who knows neither Time nor error, and under
Whose eye, unforgiving, the world, unforgiven, swings
Into shadow.

                    Long now,
The last thrush is still, the last bat
Now cruises in his sharp hieroglyphics. His wisdom
Is ancient, too, and immense. The star
Is steady, like Plato, over the mountain.

If there were no wind we might, we think, hear
The earth grind on its axis, or history
Drip in darkness like a leaking pipe in the cellar.

Rather Like a Dream

If Wordsworth, a boy, reached out
To touch stone or tree to confirm
His own reality, that wasn't

So crazy. Or even illogical. For
We have all done the same, or at least
Felt the impulse. Right now I feel it, for

I walk in the mountain woods,
Alone, hour sunset, season
When the first maple leaf falls red, the first

Beech leaf gold. Each leaf of each species
Gathers, brooding, beneath it, its film
Of darkness, and waits, and the promise

Of another summer is already a dream. Thus years,
As I stand at this moment, are gathered
In their brooding darkness beneath.

Another summer is now truly a dream
To join those moments, and hours, of joy
That dissolve into glitter, like tears, then gather

Each under a brooding leaf, or join
The darkness of conifers, not yet snow-draped.
I stand on stone and am thinking

Of what is no more. Oh, happiness!—often
Unrecognized. But shade hardens, and years
Are darkening under each leaf—old love, old folly,

Old evil and anguish, and the drawstring
Of darkness draws tighter, and the monk-hood
Of darkness grows like a sky over all,

As I stand in the spruce-deep where stars never come.
I stand, hands at sides, and wonder,
Wonder if I should put out a hand to touch

Tree or stone—just to know.

Heart of Autumn

Wind finds the northwest gap, fall comes.
Today, under gray cloud-scud and over gray
Wind-flicker of forest, in perfect formation, wild geese
Head for a land of warm water, the *boom*, the lead pellet.

Some crumple in air, fall. Some stagger, recover control,
Then take the last glide for a far glint of water. None
Knows what has happened. Now, today, watching
How tirelessly *V* upon *V* arrows the season's logic,

Do I know my own story? At least, they know
When the hour comes for the great wing-beat. Sky-strider,
Star-strider—they rise, and the imperial utterance,
Which cries out for distance, quivers in the wheeling sky.

That much they know, and in their nature know
The path of pathlessness, with all the joy
Of destiny fulfilling its own name.
I have known time and distance, but not why I am here.

Path of logic, path of folly, all
The same—and I stand, my face lifted now skyward,
Hearing the high beat, my arms outstretched in the tingling
Process of transformation, and soon tough legs,

With folded feet, trail in the sounding vacuum of passage,
And my heart is impacted with a fierce impulse
To unwordable utterance—
Toward sunset, at a great height.

from As the Dead Prey upon Us

As the dead prey upon us,
they are the dead in ourselves,
awake, my sleeping ones, I cry out to you,
disentangle the nets of being!

I pushed my car, it had been sitting so long unused.
I thought the tires looked as though they only needed air.
But suddenly the huge under body was above me,
                                                                and the rear tires
were masses of rubber and thread variously clinging together

as were the dead souls in the living room, gathered
about my mother, some of them taking care to pass
beneath the beam of the movie projector, some record
playing on the victrola, and all of them
desperate with the tawdriness of their life in hell

I turned to the young man on my right and asked, "How is it,
there?" And he begged me protestingly don't ask, we are poor
poor. And the whole room was suddenly posters
                                                                and presentations
of brake linings and other automotive accessories, cardboard
displays, the dead roaming from one to another
as bored back in life as they are in hell, poor and doomed
to mere equipments

Variations Done for Gerald Van De Wiele

I. LE BONHEUR

dogwood flakes
what is green

the petals
from the apple
blow on the road

mourning doves
mark the sway
of the afternoon, bees
dig the plum blossoms

the morning
stands up straight, the night
is blue from the full of the April moon

iris and lilac, birds
birds, yellow flowers
white flowers, the Diesel
does not let up dragging
the plow

as the whippoorwill,
the night's tractor, grinds
his song

and no other birds but us
are as busy (O saisons, o chateaux!

Délires!

What soul
is without fault?

Nobody studies
happiness

Every time the cock crows
I salute him

I have no longer any excuse
for envy. My life

has been given its orders: the seasons
seize

the soul and the body, and make mock
of any dispersed effort. The hour of death

is the only trespass

II. THE CHARGE

dogwood flakes
the green

the petals from the apple-trees
fall for the feet to walk on

the birds are so many they are
loud, in the afternoon

they distract, as so many bees do
suddenly all over the place

With spring one knows today to see
that in the morning each thing

is separate but by noon
they have melted into each other

and by night only crazy things
like the full moon and the whippoorwill

and us, are busy. We are busy
if we can get by that whiskered bird,

that nightjar, and get across, the moon
is our conversation, she will say

what soul
isn't in default?

can you afford not to make
the magical study

which happiness is? do you hear
the cock when he crows? do you know the charge

that you shall have no envy, that your life
has its orders, that the seasons

seize you too, that no body and soul are one
if they are not wrought

in this retort? that otherwise efforts
are efforts? And that the hour of your flight

will be the hour of your death?

III. SPRING

The dogwood
lights up the day.

The April moon
flakes the night.

Birds, suddenly,
are a multitude

The flowers are ravined
by bees, the fruit blossoms

are thrown to the ground, the wind
the rain forces everything. Noise—

even the night is drummed
by whippoorwills, and we get

as busy, we plow, we move,
we break out, we love. The secret

which got lost neither hides
nor reveals itself, it shows forth

tokens. And we rush
to catch up. The body

whips the soul. In its great desire
it demands the elixir

In the roar of spring,
transmutations. Envy

drags herself off. The fault of the body and the soul
—that they are not one—

the matutinal cock clangs
and singleness: we salute you

season of no bungling

Is Memory

Something we have
Or something we've lost?
How much remains of what
Happened when it first took place?
I imagine that I see you clearly,
Every detail of our first embrace,
That I still hear each word you spoke,
And the tones of your voice
As you spoke them. Yet how much
Of what comes back may be illusion,
Born of longing for what
Might later have been?

The Old Men

From way back, from when
I first came to live here
In Norfolk, I remember seeing
The old men of the village
Trudging down through the
Main street to the post office,
Or the grocery, or the pharmacy,
To get their mail or do an
Errand for the wife. Old men
Who walked slowly, some of them
With canes, they were retired
And had no place to go in any
Hurry. They would gather by twos
And threes to chew the fat
Even if there was nothing
To talk about except the weather.

Now I have a cane myself and walk
Pretty slowly, especially
If the street is icy, as it was
This morning. Young Jack Thompkins,
Mel's boy, spotted me
On the ice with my cane and
Came over to ask if he could
Help me up the steps of the
Post office. I felt a bit
Foolish but accepted his offer.
He took my arm and we made it
In good shape.

from My Aunt

Most mornings at Robin Hill
When I was living there on the
Third floor, that was before
My first marriage and when the
Office of New Directions was in
Her converted stable, she would
Summon me to her second floor
Sitting room after breakfast and
Sit me down by the fireplace for the
Daily monologue which usually
Went on for at least an hour,
Without interruption for I wasn't
Expected to say anything, just to
Listen and absorb her wisdom about
Life, of which there was a large
Supply. This sounds very boring
But it wasn't; it was endlessly
Fascinating. How had nature or
Some divine agent packed into
This little woman (she was my
Father's sister) such an intensity
Of feeling and such a capaciousness
Of spirit. She would have been in
Her sixties then and there she sat
In her Chinese silk peignoir
At the little table by the window
That looked out over the gardens
(She had attended a horticultural
School; in those days young ladies
Were not sent to college). There,
She looked out at her beautiful gardens,
After she had finished her breakfast
Which consisted only of one uncooked
Egg which she downed in a gulp.
There I was, slumped in an easy
Chair (I was forbidden to smoke
In her presence) waiting for the
Lesson to begin, impatient to have
It over so I could get on with my

Writing but curious to know what
Would come from the lips of the
Oracle that day. And once she began
I was in thrall to her conviction.

These scholia took place long, long
Ago. My aunt has been dead for over
Thirty years. The great house and
Its gardens have passed out of the
Family. I am older than she was
When she was my teacher. Yet even
Now as I sit here typing, her figure
Is as clear as if she were still
Alive; she is standing in the doorway
Of my study, the not beautiful little
Woman with the insistent voice.
Her consuming love for me has
Penetrated time, it surrounds me
Like a sacred aura. She had great
Need of me, imperfect as I was.
She had no children of her own,
And I was named for the father
Whom she idolized. I was the
Receptacle. She was determined to put
As much of him into me as she could.

She had a store of stories to tell me
About her parents and the aunts and
Uncles, even about my great-grandfather,
Who looks so fierce in the daguerreotypes
In the family album; about his house
Where wide lawns sloped down to the
Allegheny River as it came through
Pittsburgh to join the Monongahela
To make the Ohio at the Point where
Once Fort Duquesne had stood. Trips
In the buggy with her father to the
New mills on the South Side, where the
Eliza Furnaces were named for one of
Her aunts, the flames rising out of
Them against the sky at night.

What the Pencil Writes

Often when I go out I
put in my coat pocket

some paper and a pen-
cil in case I want to

write something down
well there they are

wherever I go and as
my coat moves the pen-

cil writes by itself
a kind of gibberish

hieroglyphic which I
often think as I un-

dress at night and take
out those papers with

nothing written on
them but strange &

meaningless marks is
the story of my life.

The Open Sea

We say the sea is lonely; better say
Ourselves are lonesome creatures whom the sea
Gives neither yes nor no for company.

Oh, there are people, all right, settled in the sea—
It is as populous as Maine today—
But no one who will give you the time of day.

A man who asks there of his family
Or a friend or teacher gets a cold reply
Or finds him dead against that vast majority.

Nor does it signify that people who stay
Very long, bereaved or not, at the edge of the sea
Hear the drowned folk call: that is mere fancy,

They are speechless. And the famous noise of sea,
Which a poet has beautifully told us in our day,
Is hardly a sound to speak comfort to the lonely.

Although not yet a man given to prayer, I pray
For each creature lost since the start at sea,
And give thanks it was not I, nor yet one close to me.

The Wreck of the Thresher

(Lost at Sea, April 10, 1963)

I stand on the ledge where rock runs into the river
As the night turns brackish with morning, and mourn the drowned.
Here the sea is diluted with river; I watch it slaver
Like a dog curing of rabies. Its ravening over,
Lickspittle ocean nuzzles the dry ground.
(But the dream that woke me was worse than the sea's gray
Slip-slap; there are no such sounds by day.)

This crushing of people is something we live with.
Daily, by unaccountable whim
Or caught up in some harebrained scheme of death,
Tangled in cars, dropped from the sky, in flame,
Men and women break the pledge of breath:
And now under water, gone all jetsam and small
In the pressure of oceans collected, a squad of brave men in a hull.

(Why can't our dreams be content with the terrible facts?
The only animal cursed with responsible sleep,
We trace disaster always to our own acts.
I met a monstrous self trapped in the black deep:
All these years, he smiled, *I've drilled at sea*
For this crush of water. Then he saved only me.)

We invest ships with life. Look at a harbor
At first light: with better grace than men
In their movements the vessels run to their labors
Working the fields that the tide has made green again;
Their beauty is womanly, they are named for ladies and queens,
Although by a wise superstition these are called
After fish, the finned boats, silent and submarine.
The crushing of any ship has always been held
In dread, like a house burned or a great tree felled.

I think of how sailors laugh, as if cold and wet
And dark and lost were their private, funny derision
And I can judge then what dark compression
Astonishes them now, their sunken faces set
Unsmiling, where the currents sluice to and fro
And without humor, somewhere northeast of here and below.

(Sea-brothers, I lower to you the ingenuity of dreams,
Strange lungs and bells to escape in; let me stay aboard last—
We amend our dreams in half-sleep. Then it seems
Easy to talk to the severe dead and explain the past.
Now they are saying, *Do not be ashamed to stay alive,*
You have dreamt nothing that we do not forgive.
And gentlier, *Study something deeper than yourselves,*
As, how the heart, when it turns diver, delves and saves.)

Whether we give assent to this or rage
Is a question of temperament and does not matter.
Some will has been done past our understanding,
Past our guilt surely, equal to our fears.
Dullards, we are set again to the cryptic blank page
Where the sea schools us with terrible water.
The noise of a boat breaking up and its men is in our ears.
The bottom here is too far down for our sounding;
The ocean was salt before we crawled to tears.

Winter Verse for His Sister

Moonlight washes the west side of the house
As clean as bone, it carpets like a lawn
The stubbled field tilting eastward
Where there is no sign yet of dawn.
The moon is an angel with a bright light sent
To surprise me once before I die
With the real aspect of things.
It holds the light steady and makes no comment.

Practicing for death I have lately gone
To that other house
Where our parents did most of their dying,
Embracing and not embracing their conditions.
Our father built bookcases and little by little stopped reading,
Our mother cooked proud meals for common mouths.
Kindly, they raised two children. We raked their leaves
And cut their grass, we ate and drank with them.
Reconciliation was our long work, not all of it joyful.

Now outside my own house at a cold hour
I watch the noncommittal angel lower
The steady lantern that's worn these clapboards thin
In a wash of moonlight, while men slept within,
Accepting and not accepting their conditions,
And the fingers of trees piled a deep carpet of decay
On the gravel web underneath the field,
And the field tilting always toward day.

Here and There

for Sylvia Shelly

> Whose spirit is this? we said, because we knew
> It was the spirit that we sought and knew
> That we should ask this often as she sang.
> —*Wallace Stevens, "The Idea of Order at Key West"*

I

Here in the north, a cold gray morning
does not deter the still-mating birds:
two orioles, a wood thrush? I'm not good
at this quick argot, so particular
but sounding all alike to a foreigner.
There's no heat in the house of course in May
unless I light a fire. Stevens
I think would have lighted one today
and, comfortable with my betters, I do too.

II

There in Key West, the singer lies asleep,
perhaps under a fan, after playing late
at the café. They kept her playing and singing
by the edge of the warm gulf
(after she'd watched the sun drop into it,
staying to cup Hesperus in her small hands
against the wind that rises suddenly then,
until his flame caught)—they wouldn't let her stop
at one o'clock. Now the current
runs past the island very fast
as if in panic. But the trees flower
calmly in the heat outside her house.

III

Now there are whole mindfuls of climate
in Connecticut and Florida, ideas
of moisture and drought, cold and hot—
living and dead, for that matter.
Think of how many ideas are dancing in pairs.
The idea of Wallace Stevens dancing alone
is picked up and held in mind briefly,
here and there, like a birdcall. What
is the difference between ourselves and ghosts?
Only that we move awkwardly through the air.

IV

While my cold birds chirrup—I dare not say mindlessly—
in Connecticut, and the crackling on the hearth
begins to warm me, I hear as well
the tart music of last night in the piano bar
glassed in from the green-lighted water off Key West,
the laughter struck with certain resonances
that is Sylvia's particular call,
though I think she is still asleep,
perhaps with a ceiling fan turning slowly
above her bed, between two ideas, a gulf and an ocean.

In Trackless Woods

In trackless woods, it puzzled me to find
Four great rock maples seemingly aligned,
As if they had been set out in a row
Before some house a century ago,
To edge the property and lend some shade.
I looked to see if ancient wheels had made
Old ruts to which the trees ran parallel,
But there were none, so far as I could tell—
There'd been no roadway. Nor could I find the square
Depression of a cellar anywhere,
And so I tramped on further, to survey
Amazing patterns in a hornbeam spray
Or spirals in a pine cone, under trees
Not subject to our stiff geometries.

In the Field

This field-grass brushed our legs
Last night, when out we stumbled looking up,
Wading as through the cloudy dregs
Of a wide, sparkling cup,

Our thrown-back heads aswim
In the grand, kept appointments of the air,
Save where a pine at the sky's rim
Took something from the Bear.

Black in her glinting chains,
Andromeda feared nothing from the seas,
Preserved as by no hero's pains,
Or hushed Euripides',

And there the dolphin glowed,
Still flailing through a diamond froth of stars,
Flawless as when Arion rode
One of its avatars.

But none of that was true.
What shapes that Greece or Babylon discerned
Had time not slowly drawn askew
Or like cat's cradles turned?

And did we not recall
That Egypt's north was in the Dragon's tail?
As if a form of type should fall
And dash itself like hail,

The heavens jumped away,
Bursting the cincture of the zodiac,
Shot flares with nothing left to say
To us, not coming back

Unless they should at last,
Like hard-flung dice that ramble out the throw,
Be gathered for another cast.
Whether that might be so

We could not say, but trued
Our talk awhile to words of the real sky,
Chatting of class or magnitude,
Star-clusters, nebulae,

And how Antares, huge
As Mars' big roundhouse swing, and more, was fled
As in some rimless centrifuge
Into a blink of red.

It was the nip of fear
That told us when imagination caught
The feel of what we said, came near
The schoolbook thoughts we thought,

And faked a scan of space
Blown black and hollow by our spent grenade,
All worlds dashed out without a trace,
The very light unmade.

Then, in the late-night chill,
We turned and picked our way through outcrop stone
By the faint starlight, up the hill
To where our bed-lamp shone.

Today, in the same field,
The sun takes all, and what could lie beyond?
Those holes in heaven have been sealed
Like rain-drills in a pond,

And we, beheld in gold,
See nothing starry but these galaxies
Of flowers, dense and manifold,
Which lift about our knees—

White daisy-drifts where you
Sink down to pick an armload as we pass,
Sighting the heal-all's minor blue
In chasms of the grass,

And strews of hawkweed where,
Amongst the reds or yellows as they burn,
A few dead polls commit to air
The seeds of their return.

We could no doubt mistake
These flowers for some answer to that fright
We felt for all creation's sake
In our dark talk last night,

Taking to heart what came
Of the heart's wish for life, which, staking here
In the least field an endless claim,
Beats on from sphere to sphere

And pounds beyond the sun,
Where nothing less peremptory can go,
And is ourselves, and is the one
Unbounded thing we know.

Advice to a Prophet

When you come, as you soon must, to the streets of our city,
Mad-eyed from stating the obvious,
Not proclaiming our fall but begging us
In God's name to have self-pity,

Spare us all word of the weapons, their force and range,
The long numbers that rocket the mind;
Our slow, unreckoning hearts will be left behind,
Unable to fear what is too strange.

Nor shall you scare us with talk of the death of the race.
How should we dream of this place without us?—
The sun mere fire, the leaves untroubled about us,
A stone look on the stone's face?

Speak of the world's own change. Though we cannot conceive
Of an undreamt thing, we know to our cost
How the dreamt cloud crumbles, the vines are blackened by frost,
How the view alters. We could believe,

If you told us so, that the white-tailed deer will slip
Into perfect shade, grown perfectly shy,
The lark avoid the reaches of our eye,
The jack-pine lose its knuckled grip

On the cold ledge, and every torrent burn
As Xanthus once, its gliding trout
Stunned in a twinkling. What should we be without
The dolphin's arc, the dove's return,

These things in which we have seen ourselves and spoken?
Ask us, prophet, how we shall call
Our natures forth when that live tongue is all
Dispelled, that glass obscured or broken

In which we have said the rose of our love and the clean
Horse of our courage, in which beheld
The singing locust of the soul unshelled,
And all we mean or wish to mean.

Ask us, ask us whether with the worldless rose
Our hearts shall fail us; come demanding
Whether there shall be lofty or long standing
When the bronze annals of the oak-tree close.

"A World Without Objects Is a Sensible Emptiness"

The tall camels of the spirit
Steer for their deserts, passing the last groves loud
With the sawmill shrill of the locust, to the whole honey of the arid
Sun. They are slow, proud,

And move with a stilted stride
To the land of sheer horizon, hunting Traherne's
Sensible emptiness, there where the brain's lantern-slide
Revels in vast returns.

O connoisseurs of thirst,
Beasts of my soul who long to learn to drink
Of pure mirage, those prosperous islands are accurst
That shimmer on the brink

Of absence; auras, lustres,
And all shinings need to be shaped and borne.
Think of those painted saints, capped by the early masters
With bright, jauntily worn

Aureate plates, or even
Merry-go-round rings. Turn, O turn
From the fine sleights of the sand, from the long empty oven
Where flames in flamings burn

Back to the trees arrayed
In bursts of glare, to the halo-dialing run
Of the country creeks, and the hills' bracken tiaras made
Gold in the sunken sun,

Wisely watch for the sight
Of the supernova burgeoning over the barn,
Lampshine blurred in the steam of beasts, the spirit's right
Oasis, light incarnate.

The Beautiful Changes

One wading a Fall meadow finds on all sides
The Queen Anne's Lace lying like lilies
On water; it glides
So from the walker, it turns
Dry grass to a lake, as the slightest shade of you
Valleys my mind in fabulous blue Lucernes.

The beautiful changes as a forest is changed
By a chameleon's tuning his skin to it;
As a mantis, arranged
On a green leaf, grows
Into it, makes the leaf leafier, and proves
Any greenness is deeper than anyone knows.

Your hands hold roses always in a way that says
They are not only yours; the beautiful changes
In such kind ways,
Wishing ever to sunder
Things and things' selves for a second finding, to lose
For a moment all that it touches back to wonder.

The Sound of Snow

Snow falls in the dusk of Connecticut. The stranger
Looks up to the glutenous sky, and it is remembrance
That tickles the end of his nose like the fingertips
Of a child and remembrance that touches the end of his
Tongue with the antique purity and coolness of the snow,
As if this were almost the beginning, the first snowstorm
Fluttering between his house and the serious hemlocks.

And best of all is the sound of snow in the stillness,
A susurration, the minute percussion of settling flakes;
And the stranger listens, intent to the whispering snow
In the fir boughs, earth's most intimate confiding,
And he thinks that this is the time of sweet cognizance
As it was once when the house, graying in old dusk,
Knew him and sang to him, before the house forgot.

In the last moments of day the earth and the sky
Close in the veils of snow that flutter around him,
Shutting him in the sphere of the storm, where he stands
In his elephantine galoshes, peering this way and that
At the trees in their aloofness and the nameless house
Vanishing into the dark; and he stamps his feet urgently
Turning as if in anger away from an evil companion.

Yet when, like a warning just at the fall of darkness,
Yellow light cries from the window above the house,
From the boy's room, from the old sixteen-paned window,
The stranger remembers the boy who sits in the light
And turns the glass sphere, watching to see the snowstorm
Whirling inside. And the stranger shivers and listens
To the tranquil and lucid whispering of the snow.

Stepping Backward

I waken and
    lean and look out
        to see the darkness
flee,
    sunken westward
        over curving earth,
departed
    like the long ocean
        running in tide
so fast and far
    it can never return
        or darken
this wide shore.

The last green star
    dies
        and the trees
lean in their green leaves
    westward
        as if in yearning
and then they straighten.

I rise
    from my window
        thinking now

the new words I must say
    as I step backward
        into day.

The Mythology of Dark and Light

THE FIRST VERSION

New England is a region of the heart
where she has lived always, artist
of Jahweh's unnameable burden! The forest

is cosmopolis. She wanders, a stranger
to its cantabile of green, knowing no
surprises, among beings who bear time

as they must, showing forth their changes,
the rapid, the slow. Sunlight and leaves
in combinations so various they might be

trivial, though they are not, make a dappling
of light and dark. She encounters,
without concern, a ruin. New England

is a region of common remains. Stone
that was hand-hewn, not quite square,
raises the lip of a foundation

on an old cellar-hole, all trace
of timbers gone. From the deep center
a birch swells, whitely tumescent

in a fringe of ferns. She is incurious
but gratified, and she looks intrepidly in,
walking around the ruin's emerging newness,

studying curves, angles, planes, a possible
portfolio. Not far away in the decayed orchard
is a well covered with two capstones,

worn granite and a chink between. She stands,
kneels, goes down with her palms
on the coolness. She stares into darkness

that is nothing but black, the whole of color,
down into the reverberating density
of all essence, meaning with no design,

to the wink of light there, glittering. It is
immensely distant, unimaginably close.
Perception floats on a pencil point

that leaves no mark, no line. When she stands
she knows the inexpressible that she has always
known, the zoom of the absolute

in resonances of delight and nausea,
the place of ruin, the place of renewal,
and she walks away in the traffic of the trees.

THE SECOND VERSION

When I went looking for you
  in the place of darkness that was like a house
I came first to the voices I could not see
  in discourse of great importance
to me, to everyone
  as if I were hearing waves wash along a shore
on a telephone, having dialed the wrong number.
  There was movement, there was a smell
of stale grapefruit, coffee grounds, and wine.
  Everything seemed in one sense quite ordinary,
yet I could see nothing, nothing at all.
  The voices were serious, deliberative,
perhaps argumentative,
  and when I recognized you
(by the perfume of woodsmoke you have for me alone)
  you were reluctant to leave,
you were tense and you pretended to be shy,
  by which I knew that you would not tell me
what I failed to understand.
  But you came with me, even so.
You came behind me across stony floors
  past objects like large sponges or sharks,
the sofas and other furniture of that house,
  until we arrived at the place of twilight
where at last I could see you
  and where you could see me.
You stopped, you smiled—I think wistfully—
  and you turned back.

Since then I have stayed in this back garden
like a furtive thief
lurking in the camouflage of the ivied wall,
watching the light
fall on the green hills far away
and thinking of you.

THE THIRD VERSION

Urashima, the fisher boy, was abroad on the sea
when a girl who has no name in the story
came to his boat. So lovely was she
that when she invited him to go with her
he went—and found himself far in the depths
of darkness undersea, before an obscure palace
more impressive than any dwelling one can imagine.
Urashima and the girl lived together there
for three years in untroubled happiness, surpassing
anything he had ever known or suspected,
but then the fisher boy grew homesick.
"All right," said the girl with no name,
"here is a sacred casket that will take you safely home,
but only if you promise never to open it.
Promise?" "Yes," said Urashima. And it was so,
the casket floated him safely home,
but there, amazed, he found everything changed,
his parents dead, their house gone,
whole villages where once the fields had lain empty,
and Urashima soon discovered
that he had been away not three but three hundred years.
He was devastated. He went down to the beach
and looked into the ocean's darkness
but could see nothing. Perhaps, he thought,
if I open the casket . . . He opened it,
and at once a wisp of white smoke
came from it and trailed across the sea
and then the casket was empty.
It was a long instant, there on the bright coast
of Japan, while Urashima changed
through all the ages of man; his hair turned white
and then fell out; his belly sagged

and then grew gaunt; and for a second
he was an old man hundreds of years old.
Bright sun was on the bright sand. A shriveled
man-corpse lay like the shell of a crab.

THE FOURTH VERSION

In less than half-light
when shadow
clings to the room,
in the late hour when darkness
flows from the forest
to the meadow,
nevertheless a light rises
in the bone, rises also
out in the field, in the glinting
glacial stone
that makes points of surety
in the unreliable dark.
So fine the sculptured light
on the pillow
and the gleam out in the earth
that they seem beautiful,
as if beauty were an absolute,
a design
in the dark unchanging depths
of light. Is it so or not?
Is it worse if the fine small light
is beauty only by inference
of joy or praise
in the need of the night?
To have seen it is something.
Imagination can do that
in stone or bone.
But to have raised it, roused it
in the face
is more than imagination can do
alone. The rest is the power
most clearly ours, most human
and the best.

His Dream
Raspberry thickets leaping, splashing
on the barrier of old stone, remnant
of a prior civilization, where she rises
with light streaming from her flanks
and stands half-turned, the she-bear
born from the oceanic earth that still
darkens her eyes;
                                        stands in the might
of her sex, poised, uncertain, waiting.
Then she comes to him, touches him,
rubs herself against him, and he longs
to embrace her but his limbs are wooden,
he cries out in an anguish of rustling,
his heart thuds under his ribs of bark.

Her Dream
Secret amusement, the inward smile
she cherishes alone while she walks
among huge geometric shapes,
spheres and pyramids, mile upon mile
in the glare of the intense plain.
Motorcycles race past her, ridden
by singleminded men with flames
fluttering from naked shoulders.
She steps from shadow to shadow.
Hot light and the din of motors—
how absurd. She waves to a cyclist
who gapes in amazement and races on.
In the shadow of a sphere she finds
an abandoned machine, the frame,
the wheels and handlebars, but no
motor. She mounts it, her back curved
the smooth heaviness between her thighs,
and with a power generated inside her,
a power gratifying beyond expectation,
she glides forward, swifter than all,
in the cool wind, in the silence.

It will come to be, but only when the myth
functionally ceases, of course. Dark and light.
Clear as black and white, or as day and night.
Folk wisdom always rhymes because what we call
wisdom is the mediating of opposites. Total
presence, total absence. All color, no color.
Remember, ours is the animal eye, not dark,
not light, but juice merely, merely transparency.
Further it is tempting to say that she, the painter,
sees from the dark toward the light and that he,
the poet, sees from the light toward the dark, but that
would be an oversimplification. Perhaps our trouble
is that we no longer can be satisfied
with oversimplification. One knows
such agonies, forceful conciliations! Kodály's
duo for light and dark (violin & cello, Op. 7)
(the agonies, too, of Heifetz and Piatigorsky), or
Vlaminck's Bridge at Chatou or that extraordinary
seizing-up of soul in The Road. At all events
though we struggle, and know we must struggle,
to retain our relativism, our mediating belief,
the two absolutes are unassailable. All and nothing.
Hence they resolve dangerously into one. Sometimes
god, vindictive and helpless, or destination,
the all too unmetaphysical injustice; but
for us the myth is $E = MC^2$. Ever more difficult,
more dangerous, less satisfying, this human function
which we call consciousness. Trying to make
ends meet (and the solace of facetiae). No wonder
so many drop out. Can one blame them? Yet each
defection brings us nearer to loss of function,
the time before and after myth, called Chaos.
"Ah," they cry out, such dear people, she and he.
"How can we continue? It is too hard. Too hard. . . ."

A Tenancy

for David Jackson

Something in the light of this March afternoon
Recalls that first and dazzling one
Of 1946. I sat elated
In my old clothes, in the first of several
Furnished rooms, head cocked for the kind of sound
That is recognized only when heard.
A fresh snowfall muffled the road, unplowed
To leave blanker and brighter
The bright, blank page turned overnight.

A yellow pencil in midair
Kept sketching unfamiliar numerals,
The 9 and 6 forming a stereoscope
Through which to seize the Real
Old-Fashioned Winter of my landlord's phrase,
Through which the ponderous *idées reçues*
Of oak, velour, crochet, also the mantel's
Baby figures, value told me
In some detail at the outset, might be plumbed
For signs I should not know until I saw them.

But the objects, innocent
(As we all once were) of annual depreciation
The more I looked grew shallower,
Pined under a luminous plaid robe
Thrown over us by the twin mullions, sashes,
And unequal oblong panes
Of windows and storm windows. These,
Washed in a rage, then left to dry unpolished,
Projected onto the inmost wall
Ghosts of the storm, like pebbles under water.

And indeed, from within, ripples
Of heat had begun visibly bearing up and away
The bouquets and wreaths of a quarter century.
Let them go, what did I want with them?
It was time to change that wallpaper!
Brittle, sallow in the new radiance,
Time to set the last wreath floating out
Above the dead, to sweep up flowers. The dance
Had ended, it was light; the men looked tired
And awkward in their uniforms.
I sat, head thrown back, and with the dried stains
Of light on my own cheeks, proposed
This bargain with—say with the source of light:
That given a few years more
(Seven or ten or, what seemed vast, fifteen)
To spend in love, in a country not at war,
I would give in return
All I had. All? A little sun
Rose in my throat. The lease was drawn.

I did not even feel the time expire.

I feel it though, today, in this new room,
Mine, with my things and thoughts, a view
Of housetops, treetops, the walls bare.
A changing light is deepening, is changing
To a gilt ballroom chair a chair
Bound to break under someone before long.
I let the light change also me.
The body that lived through that day
And the sufficient love and relative peace
Of those short years, is now not mine.
Would it be called a soul?
It knows, at any rate,
That when the light dies and the bell rings
Its leaner veteran will rise to face
Partners not recognized
Until drunk young again and gowned in changing
Flushes; and strains will rise,
The bone-tipped baton beating, rapid, faint,
From the street below, from my depressions—

From the doorbell which rings.
One foot asleep, I hop
To let my three friends in. They stamp
Themselves free of the spring's
Last snow—or so we hope.

One has brought violets in a pot;
The second, wine; the best,
His open, empty hand. Now in the room
The sun is shining like a lamp.
I put the flowers where I need them most

And then, not asking why they come,
Invite the visitors to sit.
If I am host at last
It is of little more than my own past.
May others be at home in it.

The Emerald

Hearing that on Sunday I would leave,
My mother asked if we might drive downtown.
Why certainly—off with my dressing gown!
The weather had turned fair. *We* were alive.

Only the gentle General she married
Late, for both an old way out of harm's,
Fought for breath, surrendered in her arms,
With military honors now lay buried.

That week the arcana of his medicine chest
Had been disposed of, and his clothes. Gold belt
Buckle and the letter from President Roosevelt
Went to an unknown grandchild in the West.

Downtown, his widow raised her parasol
Against the Lenten sun's not yet detectable
Malignant atomies which an electric needle
Unfreckles from her soft white skin each fall.

Hence too her chiffon scarf, pale violet,
And spangle-paste dark glasses. Each spring we number
The new dead. Above ground, who can remember
Her as she once was? Even I forget,

Fail to attend her, seem impervious . . .
Meanwhile we have made through a dense shimmy
Of parked cars burnished by the midday chamois
For Mutual Trust. Here cool gloom welcomes us,

And all, director, guard, quite palpably
Adore her. Spinster tellers one by one
Darting from cages, sniffling to meet her son,
Think of her having a son—! She holds the key

Whereby palatial bronze gates shut like jaws
On our descent into this inmost vault.
The keeper bends his baldness to consult,
Brings a tin box painted mud-brown, withdraws.

She opens it. Security. Will. Deed.
Rummages further. Rustle of tissue, a sprung
Lid. Her face gone queerly lit, fair, young,
Like faces of our dear ones who have died.

No rhinestone now, no dilute amethyst,
But of the first water, linking star to pang,
Teardrop to fire, my father's kisses hang
In lipless concentration round her wrist.

Gray are these temple-drummers who once more
Would rouse her, girl-bride jeweled in his grave.
Instead, she next picks out a ring. "He gave
Me this when you were born. Here, take it for—

For when you marry. For your bride. It's yours."
A den of greenest light, it grows, shrinks, glows,
Hermetic stanza bedded in the prose
Of the last thirty semiprecious years.

I do not tell her, it would sound theatrical,
Indeed this green room's mine, my very life.
We are each other's; there will be no wife;
The little feet that patter here are metrical.

But onto her worn knuckle slip the ring.
Wear it for me, I silently entreat,
Until—until the time comes. Our eyes meet.
The world beneath the world is brightening.

The Victor Dog

for Elizabeth Bishop

Bix to Buxtehude to Boulez,
The little white dog on the Victor label
Listens long and hard as he is able.
It's all in a day's work, whatever plays.

From judgment, it would seem, he has refrained.
He even listens earnestly to Bloch,
Then builds a church upon our acid rock.
He's man's—no—he's the Leiermann's best friend,

Or would be if hearing and listening were the same.
Does he hear? I fancy he rather smells
Those lemon-gold arpeggios in Ravel's
"Les jets d'eau du palais de ceux qui s'aiment."

He ponders the Schumann Concerto's tall willow hit
By lightning, and stays put. When he surmises
Through one of Bach's eternal boxwood mazes
The oboe pungent as a bitch in heat,

Or when the calypso decants its raw bay rum
Or the moon in *Wozzeck* reddens ripe for murder,
He doesn't sneeze or howl; just listens harder.
Adamant needles bear down on him from

Whirling of outer space, too black, too near—
But he was taught as a puppy not to flinch,
Much less to imitate his bête noire Blanche
Who barked, fat foolish creature, at King Lear.

Still others fought in the road's filth over Jezebel,
Slavered on hearths of horned and pelted barons.
His forebears lacked, to say the least, forbearance.
Can nature change in him? Nothing's impossible.

The last chord fades. The night is cold and fine.
His master's voice rasps through the grooves' bare groves.
Obediently, in silence like the grave's
He sleeps there on the still-warm gramophone

Only to dream he is at the première of a Handel
Opera long thought lost—*Il Cane Minore*.
Its allegorical subject is his story!
A little dog revolving round a spindle

Gives rise to harmonies beyond belief,
A cast of stars . . . Is there in Victor's heart
No honey for the vanquished? Art is art.
The life it asks of us is a dog's life.

from Mirabell: Books of Number

Sun is rising. The cool, smalltown dawn!
Now through gently breathing shades it strums
The brass bed, a quick bar or two, and the long,
Hushed day—August 21st—begins
By whose unthinkable finale we
(However often, faced with splendors, left
Dutifully rapt—until, made "ours,"
Pressed in a freshman Plato like wildflowers,
The mummied angel slumbered) may for once
Find this pure dew of expectancy
Undried upon the skin. The hours change
Clothes in silence. Noon. No letters. One.
A highlight excommunicates the phone.
Things look out at us as from a spell
They themselves have woven. Young, windblown
Maria with dark glasses and Gitane—
Snapshot tucked in the mirror. Book by Wystan
Face up among the clouds and bats, all week
Open to Miranda's villanelle.
Tin bird at attention by the salt.
The salt-cellar in its own right, a bisque
Egg one shy bluebell embellishes,
Found when we moved here, eldest of this troupe
Brought up to interact, to shrug off risk
At any level. Three. The hands that halt
Second by second coming round ablaze
—*Crack!* Like a walnut, only louder. Did—?
Who first, in this red room, saw nothing now
See nothing else: our baby pyramid
Overexcited, split along its flawed
Fire escapes to spectral rubble . . . Well,
Something had to give. And will light learn
To modify its power before our turn?
We humbly hope so. Four. No further sign
Of who approaches, or of his design—
Only the radiance inching into place.

By five the breath indrawn is held and held.

The world was everything that was the case?
Open the case. Lift out the fabulous
Necklace, in form a spiral molecule
Whose sparklings outmaneuver time, space, us.
Here where the table glistens, cleared, one candle
Shines invisibly in the slant light
Beside our nameless houseplant. It's the hour
When Hell (a syllable identified
In childhood as the German word for *bright*
—So that my father's cheerful "Go to Hell,"
Long unheard, and Vaughan's unbeatable
"They are all gone into a world of light"
Come, even now at times, to the same thing)—
The hour when Hell shall render what it owes.
Render to whom? how? What at this late date
Can be done with the quaint idiom that slips
From nowhere to my tongue—or from the parchment
Of some old scribe of the apocalypse—
But render *it* as the long rendering to
Light of this very light stored by our cells
These past five million years, these past five minutes
Here by the window, taking in through panes
Still bleary from the hurricane a gull's
Ascending aureole of decibels,
As numberless four-pointed brilliancies
Upon the Sound's mild silver grid come, go?
The message hardly needs decoding, so
Sheer the text, so innocent and fleet
These overlapping pandemonia:
Birdlife, leafplay, rockface, waterglow
Lending us their being, till the given
Moment comes to render what we owe.

Dead Center

Upon reflection, as I dip my pen
Tonight, forth ripple messages in code.
In Now's black waters burn the stars of Then.

Seen from the embankment, marble men
Sleep upside down, bat-wise, the sleep bestowed
Upon reflection. As I dip my pen

Think how others, deeper into Zen,
Blew on immediacy until it glowed,
In Now's black waters burn the stars of Then.

Or else I'm back at Grandmother's. I'm ten,
Dust hides my parents' roadster from the road
Which dips—*into* reflection, with my pen.

Breath after breath, harsh O's of oxygen—
Never deciphered, what do they forebode?
In Now's black waters burn the stars. Ah then

Leap, Memory, supreme equestrienne,
Through hoops of fire, circuits you overload!
Beyond reflection, as I dip my pen
In Now's black waters, burn the stars of Then.

Night River

The heavy river winds around
the foot of the wharf. Gasoline ribbons
like rainbow eels flutter on its brown
slow-changing face. Oranges and condoms
drifting under the pilings whorl
through its eyes past the warehouse docks
of big ships and the vacant piers where jock-
strapped boys swim in the Hudson, the Charles,
the Connecticut, the Platte, the great
streams of national culture, the states'
pride, the navigable ways of the world.

On the other bank, a drunken girl
rises on to her elbow; a dog
urinates on a tree; a log
rolls on to the beach reserved for summer.

The river has no street or number.
It cannot keep faithful. Whore to the world
at our feet tonight it lies asleep
in the moonlight as softly as a girl
dreaming of lovers she cannot keep.

Identity Crisis

He was urged to prepare for success: "You never can tell,"
he was told over and over; "others have made it;
one dare not presume to predict. You never can tell.

Who's Who in America lists the order of cats
in hunting, fishing, bird-watching, farming,
domestic service—the dictionary order of cats

who have made it. Those not in the book are beyond the pale.
Not to succeed in your chosen profession is unthinkable.
Either you make it or—you're beyond the pale.

Do you understand?"
"No," he shakes his head.
"Are you ready to forage for freedom?"
"No," he adds,
"I mean, why is a cat always shaking his head?

Because he's thinking: who am I? I am not
only one-ninth myself. I always am
all of the selves I have been and will be but am not."

"The normal cat," I tell him, "soon adjusts
to others and to changing circumstances;
he makes his way the way he soon adjusts."

"I can't," he says, "perhaps because I'm blue,
big-footed, lop-eared, socially awkward, impotent,
and I drink too much, whether because I'm blue

or because I like it, who knows. I want to escape
at five o'clock into an untouchable world
where the top is the bottom and everyone wants to escape

from the middle, everyone, every day. I mean,
I have visions of two green eyes rising
out of the ocean, blinking, knowing what I mean."

"Never mind the picture, repeat after me
the self's creed. What he tells you you
tells me and I repeats. Now, after me:

I love myself, I wish I would live well.
Your gift of love breaks through my self-defeat.
All prizes are blue. No cat admits defeat.
The next time that he lives he will live well."

Watersong

When I spend a long time fishing alone,
the brook begins to sing
as if a cemetery of souls in the stones
were rising in a ring
around me, like a hatch of mayflies,
exulting, then fleeing to the woods.

Why insects are so small is not surprising:
fact is they have no bones.
What do they make of the moon's rising
in the firs like an orange stone?
Don't my boots and my two small eyes
trespass on their livelihood?

In our last home we're all alone.
Some fear forever; some sing.
What's piously carved in the granite stones
is a joke. Amoral surroundings,
suns swarm and sink in the western skies
without being evil or doing good.

what the cranes said

Under the tall pine
    by the chinaberry
  Hurry! Hurry! The sundial has lost its shadow,
    shrieked the green cranes, *the garden is empty;*
  the mountain tilts backward; the wind is hollow;
    black ice on the pond; a scent of snow;
        the sky is red with flames
  the woeful screeching of the trees
    tells us how close the fire comes.

By the honeyed pine
    near the chinaberry
  Come! Come with me!
    the great white crane
  replied, standing tall on her long black legs.
    The molten earth waxes and wanes;
  tonight as the sun set the clouds became flames,
    mountains darkened, then Orion seized the sky;
  but now the full moon as fat as a wheel
    brings a new year round—
and she flew up and away as dark as a shadow
    over the winter ground.

Christmas Eve in Whitneyville

December, and the closing of the year;
The momentary carolers complete
Their Christmas Eves, and quickly disappear
Into their houses on each lighted street.

Each car is put away in each garage;
Each husband home from work, to celebrate,
Has closed his house around him like a cage,
And wedged the tree until the tree stood straight.

Tonight you lie in Whitneyville again,
Near where you lived, and near the woods or farms
Which Eli Whitney settled with the men
Who worked at mass-producing firearms.

The main street, which was nothing after all
Except a school, a stable, and two stores,
Was improvised and individual,
Picking its way alone, among the wars.

Now Whitneyville is like the other places,
Ranch houses stretching flat beyond the square,
Same stores and movie, same composite faces
Speaking the language of the public air.

Old houses of brown shingle still surround
This graveyard where you wept when you were ten
And helped to set a coffin in the ground.
You left a friend from school behind you then,

And now return, a man of fifty-two.
Talk to the boy. Tell him about the years
When Whitneyville quadrupled, and how you
And all his friends went on to make careers,

Had cars as long as hayracks, boarded planes
For Rome or Paris where the pace was slow
And took the time to think of how yearly gains,
Profit and volume made the business grow.

"The things I had to miss," you said last week,
"Or thought I had to, take my breath away."
You propped yourself on pillows, where your cheek
Was hollow, stubbled lightly with new gray.

This love is jail; another sets us free.
Tonight the houses and their noise distort
The thin rewards of solidarity.
The houses lean together for support.

The noises fail, and lights go on upstairs.
The men and women are undressing now
To go to sleep. They put their clothes on chairs
To take them up again. I think of how,

All over Whitneyville, when midnight comes,
They lie together and are quieted,
To sleep as children sleep, who suck their thumbs,
Cramped in the narrow rumple of each bed.

They will not have unpleasant thoughts tonight.
They make their houses jails, and they will take
No risk of freedom for the appetite,
Or knowledge of it, when they are awake.

The lights go out and it is Christmas Day.
The stones are white, the grass is black and deep.
I will go back and leave you here to stay
Where the dark houses harden into sleep.

White Apples

when my father had been dead a week
I woke
with his voice in my ear
                                                  I sat up in bed
and held my breath
and stared at the pale closed door

white apples and the taste of stone

if he called again
I would put on my coat and galoshes

Kicking the Leaves

1

Kicking the leaves, October, as we walk home together
from the game, in Ann Arbor,
on a day the color of soot, rain in the air;
I kick at the leaves of maples,
reds of seventy different shades, yellow
like old paper; and poplar leaves, fragile and pale;
and elm leaves, flags of a doomed race.
I kick at the leaves, making a sound I remember
as the leaves swirl upward from my boot,
and flutter; and I remember
Octobers walking to school in Connecticut,
wearing corduroy knickers that swished
with a sound like leaves; and a Sunday buying
a cup of cider at a roadside stand
on a dirt road in New Hampshire; and kicking the leaves,
autumn 1955 in Massachusetts, knowing
my father would die when the leaves were gone.

2

Each fall in New Hampshire, on the farm
where my mother grew up, a girl in the country,
my grandfather and grandmother
finished the autumn work, taking the last vegetables in
from the cold fields, canning, storing roots and apples
in the cellar under the kitchen. Then my grandfather
raked leaves against the house
as the final chore of autumn.
One November I drove up from college to see them.
We pulled big rakes, as we did when we hayed in summer,
pulling the leaves against the granite foundations
around the house, on every side of the house,
and then, to keep them in place, we cut spruce boughs
and laid them across the leaves,
green on red, until the house
was tucked up, ready for snow
that would freeze the leaves in tight, like a stiff skirt.

Then we puffed through the shed door,
taking off boots and overcoats, slapping our hands,
and sat in the kitchen, rocking, and drank
black coffee my grandmother made,
three of us sitting together, silent, in gray November.

3

One Saturday when I was little, before the war,
my father came home at noon from his half day at the office
and wore his Bates sweater, black on red,
with the crossed hockey sticks on it, and raked beside me
in the back yard, and tumbled in the leaves with me,
laughing, and carried me, laughing, my hair full of leaves,
to the kitchen window
where my mother could see us, and smile, and motion
to set me down, afraid I would fall and be hurt.

4

Kicking the leaves today, as we walk home together
from the game, among crowds of people
with their bright pennants, as many and bright as leaves,
my daughter's hair is the red-yellow color
of birch leaves, and she is tall like a birch,
growing up, fifteen, growing older; and my son
flamboyant as maple, twenty,
visits from college, and walks ahead of us, his step
springing, impatient to travel
the woods of the earth. Now I watch them
from a pile of leaves beside this clapboard house
in Ann Arbor, across from the school
where they learned to read,
as their shapes grow small with distance, waving,
and I know that I
diminish, not them, as I go first
into the leaves, taking
the way they will follow, Octobers and years from now.

5

This year the poems came back, when the leaves fell.
Kicking the leaves, I heard the leaves tell stories,
remembering, and therefore looking ahead, and building
the house of dying. I looked up into the maples
and found them, the vowels of bright desire.
I thought they had gone forever
while the bird sang *I love you, I love you*
and shook its black head
from side to side, and its red eye with no lid,
through years of winter, cold
as the taste of chickenwire, the music of cinderblock.

6

Kicking the leaves, I uncover the lids of graves.
My grandfather died at seventy-seven, in March
when the sap was running; and I remember my father
twenty years ago,
coughing himself to death at fifty-two in the house
in the suburbs. Oh, how we flung
leaves in the air! How they tumbled and fluttered around us,
like slowly cascading water, when we walked together
in Hamden, before the war, when Johnson's Pond
had not surrendered to houses, the two of us
hand in hand, and in the wet air the smell of leaves
burning;
and in six years I will be fifty-two.

7

Now I fall, now I leap and fall
to feel the leaves crush under my body, to feel my body
buoyant in the ocean of leaves, the night of them,
night heaving with death and leaves, rocking like the ocean.
Oh, this delicious falling into the arms of leaves,
into the soft laps of leaves!
Face down, I swim into the leaves, feathery,
breathing the acrid odor of maple, swooping
in long glides to the bottom of October—

where the farm lies curled against winter, and soup steams
its breath of onion and carrot
onto damp curtains and windows; and past the windows
I see the tall bare maple trunks and branches, the oak
with its few brown weathery remnant leaves,
and the spruce trees, holding their green.
Now I leap and fall, exultant, recovering
from death, on account of death, in accord with the dead,
the smell and taste of leaves again,
and the pleasure, the only long pleasure, of taking a place
in the story of leaves.

1943

They toughened us for war. In the high school auditorium
Ed Monahan knocked out Dominick Esposito in the first round

of the heavyweight finals, and ten months later Dom died
in the third wave at Tarawa. Every morning of the war

our Brock-Hall Dairy delivered milk from horse-drawn wagons
to wooden back porches in southern Connecticut. In winter,

frozen cream lifted the cardboard lids of glass bottles,
grade A or grade B, while Marines bled to death in the surf,

or the right engine faltered into Channel silt, or troops marched
—what could we do?—with frostbitten feet as white as milk.

An Old Song

What she and I had between us once, America
And its hope had; and just as I grieve alternately
For what I know myself to have lost of what had been,
And for all that loss I was suffering all that while
I was doing, I thought, so well, so goes the nation,
Grieving for her hope, either lost, or from the very
Start, a lost cause. All our states and I are one in this.
O my America, my long-lost land lady of
The hardening ground, the house neither ancient nor in
Good repair, the brackish stream, the half-abandoned mill,
The red plastic bucket that hung in the place we kept
By the beach where, I remember, August evenings
Rang with hilarity until we trembled with cold.

Pageant of the Cold

The Queen of the Parade floats by on her painted car,
Glitteringly, in between postures—sitting for some
Endless series of portraits? lying for the moment?
Standing for the brave Muse of Parading who could not
Make it this afternoon? Ten streets ahead The Old Men's
Band plays *A Closer Walk with Thee* as chromatic tints
Of something bouncy in another key fall across
Its dying sounds. Held down by long guy-ropes in the hands
Of struggling lackeys, the Great Forms float by overhead—
Pegasus, Apollo, a Hippogriff, Daffy Duck:
In childhood, knowing that these balloons were full of air
Deflated in no way whatever stature they had.
Now we gaze sadly, bored, at the Triumph of Moments.

But the Queen will not be forsworn. She turns her head, smiles,
And waves at us amid even more oompahs, sirens
Cutting the distant air, seducing all attention
To the violent island all around us, away
From this tacky-tawdry ill-timed progress, this parade
Of tired fables which is now an institution.
But the sirens are tired too and have all belonged
For some years to the Society of Sound Effects.
They are as part of a neighboring parade the Queen
Will also loll amidst, begrimed as beglittered now.
Her smiles go on for miles; the great balloons will preside
Over the darkening streets, over the lackeying
Layers of lower air they gravely bow and sway among.

That's for Oblivion

A day I had forgotten reappeared to me, clad
In a kind of dimmed radiance, neither presenting
Its case, nor yet asking me to represent my own,
But with an equitable air went on its errand
Of merely being there. I called out for you to come
And help me deal with it, but you were somewhere else (out
Looking across the morning water at where the next
Morning would be coming from, it now appears you were).
So that pale day waited, and on being asked in which
Of the volumes of my life it was to be inscribed,
Disappeared with the curious perfume and the most
Melodious twang so common to such vanishings.
That was when you came in with a flaming day-lily.

Collected Novels

Where does one start? Perhaps here, at the middle
Of them all, as now, with *Elevenses*, that
Strange minor afterpiece, a book of partings
And mostly written on shipboard in passage
Between a new old world and an old new one,
Rocking between a fear of open ocean
And an arrival at a terror firmer
Than that, its separate sections somehow stand
For all the other novels: one can find them
There, such as in the scene where they both promise,
Standing by the inadequate lifeboat, drunk—

But you never read that one. Perhaps you did
Guess things about the juvenilia: *The
Rock Cried Out "I'm Burning Too"* was the first one
(In England called *A Universe of Death*), long,
Lyrical, assaulted by gangs of fancies,
Burdened with epigraphs, limping earnestly
Along corridors dimly lit with callow
Candor. On the other hand, *The Book of the
Perfect Clown*, the second of my first books, with
Its mock-dialogue form, inset tales, and arch
Picaro gestures, shone with counterfeit light.

Next, *My Brother's Reaper* was a mystery.
(I'd wanted its title to be *The Case of
The Limiting Case*, avowing how here the
Solution was indeed the discovery
Of the proof that the case was insoluble.)
It was an anatomy of doubt, and the
Successful but untriumphant detective
Disappeared unexplainedly at the end,
So that his career could not continue in
Other books, but only in life. Here it stands,
In all its cheap editions, with the others.

The truth is out. You have the books: I give you
Their true authorship. You'll find among them our
Collaboration, the epistolary
Most Said, about the couple who put about
Experimental rumors of their life in
Order to trace out the modellings of truth
(Keeping safe in that the facts were notional)
By friends and lovers. And about what happened to
Them thereby (we rejected *The French Letters*
As title, with "For Prevention of Disease
Only" as epigraph—but you remember . . .)

It does belong with the others—even with
That purgatorial vision, *Peeping Tom*,
Its solipsistic opposite, lonely and
Mad in its questing for certainties of light;
The intricate *récit* of an old voyeur
Epistemologist, it tells of three
Wives, Virgilia, Matilda and Beatrice,
His three lives with them, and of his going blind
After a life of seeing wisely and far
Too well; full of long digressions on mirrors,
Cameras, pictures—not the best sort of novel.

No: the few good ones were those which went about
Their sad work of imagining marriages,
Doing what we need such texts for, providing
Models of the mysteries of pairs we are
Not part of, and mirrors of our unknown own.
Leaving, for one, and *The Right Links* and even
Merrydown, that romance of sunken heights and
Afterpleasures: broad canvases, cities and
Seaside sojourns, many households, and, that there
Be truth, humming swarms of irrelevancies—
These redeemed the early games and drawn-out songs.

The novel of wartime London, *Dark Cremorne*,
Hardly a failure, dwelt in its retractions
Of vision—squinting through magnesium glare,
Turning emptied eyes toward the cold dawn—and was
One with its minima—few characters, a
Minor rondo of fewer locales, even
The poor, grey wartime paper of the book James
Chamberlain was reading, sad food, those frightful
Knickers to be got past to delicate hairs.
Yet these simple, enviable pleasures robbed
From death seem bright idylls of denial now.

(No, *Blackbird Cross* would have been a bad title
—Taken from the bus-route terminus and, of
Course, from Helen Elizabeth's dream: you must
Have guessed by now what part you played in it.) But
About the destroyed manuscripts of what was
To have been *Jealousy* I shall say nothing.
It is not here among the works. It might have
Been the worst or the best—a vivisection
Of desperate knowledges and narrowings,
Of the sense that one's death is being kept from
One—or one's life. The earliest drafts were endless.

They are finally together on the shelf—
As if about to be packed up for moving—
Here at a somber time of dissolution,
Leaning wearily against each other: some
From out of the closet and still dusty with
Concealment, some that had been staring out at
You all along, others from scattered regions
Of the house, huddling together, refugees
Bereft if not of their titles then of their
Various makers' names—the ones in which I
Penned them (or in which I, too, was penned). All mine.

Having no terror of design, you would not
Have dreaded knowing that all these works had one
Author. But that I failed to write them under
My true name is not a matter merely for
The spirit's connoisseurship: to gather them
Here, half a dusty sheaf of hybrid grains, is
To acknowledge the too early arrival
Of frost, the race for a few last hours of light
To read by, to plant or reap by. I would have
Given you their common life: I have left you
Them, though, like eleven expired leases:

The last one, in press, being *Some Natural*
Tears, which we were to have read together, hand
In hand. You may perhaps now guess its subject—
The old story we all know and can never
Comprehend, its fierce transfers of elation
Across the bound of loss, its presentiments
Of ending, departures in the evening
Shade of sky and distant horizontal woods.
Announced in this reprint of *Elevenses*,
It shall at least reach you under my own name.

Adam's Task

And Adam gave names to all cattle, and
to the fowl of the air, and to every
beast of the field . . . *Gen. 2:20*

Thou, paw paw-paw; thou, glurd; thou, spotted
Glurd; thou, whitestap, lurching through
The high-grown brush; thou, pliant-footed,
Implex; thou, awagabu.

Every burrower, each flier
Came for the name he had to give:
Gay, first work, ever to be prior,
Not yet sunk to primitive.

Thou, verdle; thou, McFleery's pomma;
Thou; thou; thou—three types of grawl;
Thou, flisket; thou, kabasch; thou, comma-
Eared mashawk; thou, all; thou, all.

Were, in a fire of becoming,
Laboring to be burned away,
Then work, half-measuring, half-humming,
Would be as serious as play.

Thou, pambler; thou, rivarn; thou, greater
Wherret, and thou, lesser one;
Thou, sproal; thou, zant; thou, lily-eater.
Naming's over. Day is done.

Ode on St. Cecilia's Day 1964

1. OF THE PAST

Some music, then, for this day. Let it be
Suitable to the mood of fallen snow,
The veil of a virgin saint. Quietly
Let it come now, out of the silence; now
While the birds inexplicably forsake
The elm, the oak, the seed in the lilac . . . .
Instead, drumrolls muffled in an old year,
An echo of trumpets in the streets. Clear
But muted, there is a ragged tattoo
Of hooves, image of a sable horse, wild-
Eyed, resisting the rein, skittish among
The twin rows of witness citizens who,
Their voices frozen, give up to the cold
Air of the marble city an old song.

2. OF THE PRESENT

But it's another year, Cecilia's day
Again, another part of the land. So,
Let the phantoms of those dead days lie
Under these new burdens of snow. Allow
That chorus of stricken men to dim like
Shadows into blackening film, the dark
Merging with the riderless horse. Feature
By feature, let the scene fade into near
Distance, into perspective, then shadow.
This is music for St. Cecilia. Yield
To her the lyric due her. Let us sing
For her patronage—her martyrdom grew
Out of a summer heart: she is our shield
Against the winter. She is always young.

3. OF THE MOMENT

Here beyond the window the campus lies.
The students pass in mufflers and coats, eyes
Almost hidden against the wind. The sound
Of radio music settles around
The furniture, into the carpeting.
Choral voices: a requiem. Distant
And urgent, the November church bells ring.
Outdoors a dog rags something. An instant
Pause in his play—he has caught a squirrel
Which tosses and tosses in the gray air.
The mongrel, in the midst of his quarrel
With life, is assaulted by three girls. There,
At the base of a tree, the limp ruff falls
From insensate jaws, starts to inch up walls
Of oak bark toward some invisible
Sanctuary. The dog begins to howl.
The girls watch the squirrel into the limbs.
Cecilia's radio is done with hymns.

The Late, Late Show

It is now ten minutes after midnight,
December 5th, 1965. In honor
of the attack by the Japanese
on Pearl Harbor, Hawaii, on
December 7th, 1941, all channels

are running movies about war. On one
channel, the come-on is newsreel footage of the
bombing inserted into a film
made by the Japanese. Channel
9 has topped that: also Japanese, the movie is

science-fiction: the Third World War is just
beginning. I'll take a gangster film—Channel 3:
it sounds incredible, but the third
world war is already over
over here. This one is American. Let me check

the T.V. Guide: "'Five.' (1951).
The only five survivors of atomic war
revive man's ancient hostilities
and prejudices." The whole thing
is starting again. So I have turned to writing this

poem as I watch. I have survived one
Armageddon; I shall build a microcosm.
I am writing very carefully:
the woman is pregnant, and the
Negro is building a house. I want my facts to be

accurate, in case this is the last thing
to be left. The sounds do not matter, only the
sense. If you are reading this, I hope
that it will not upset you, sir,
whoever you are. It may be that my typewriter

was hocked, passed peacefully from dark shelf to
dark shelf in ancient shops until it was sold for
scrap. Grant us this: that was possible.
But if you should find this lying
rolled in my machine, the letters of our alphabet

scrambled in the dust, grant us this much more:
we foresaw the end too clearly for it to matter.

The Recurring Dream

for Luigi, in memoriam.

I seek my father—that minister
of the deep—among the furniture
of my childhood. I step out of waking
into this room and know
that time has passed. The windows are webbed
and moonstreaked. A lamp with a glass shade,

green and saffron, burns
on a brass stem. The bookcases hold sermons
and silence. My aquaria
stand among tumbled
tomes and testaments. The dust rises
into the amber darkness.

I disturb a desert of hours,
search for the fish that glide
in musty waters—blue scales
glint under my glance,
their eyes are corals budding
among rusty blades of sea grass

and swordplants. I remove the glass lids
and dip my hand into the water—
it is what I have feared:
shadow of a shadow, dim air
flowing from corner to corner.
The fish rise along the curtains

to swim about me in the air,
their black fins wavering.
I dig in the gravel stranded
among the shelving,
the decaying books. I dig,
and here, in the root

of the largest plant, blooming
from a socket of bone, I find my father
where he has scuttled,
at last to be brought back, smiling.

Wake Disturbing Surfaces

If we come by water,
hull down in dream,
our wake disturbing surfaces, but not
the dim currents where images swim and waver,
we will find the common island

and the serpents we
have set to guard
the hoards we have hidden in the deepest
caves. Then, with bone flute and the nerve-strung harp, we will
charm our serpents with scales other

than their own, and we
will plunder and
be plundered. Our ship will ride gunwale-low
over that sea whose tide rises and falls like old
music in the throat of the world.

A Chair

A chair has waited such a long time to be with its person. Through shadow and fly buzz and the floating dust it has waited such a long time to be with its person.

What it remembers of the forest it forgets, and dreams of a room where it waits—Of the cup and the ceiling—Of the Animate One.

A Stone Is Nobody's

A man ambushed a stone. Caught it. Made it a prisoner. Put it in a dark room and stood guard over it for the rest of his life.

His mother asked why.

He said, because it's held captive, because it is the captured.

Look, the stone is asleep, she said, it does not know whether it's in a garden or not. Eternity and the stone are mother and daughter, it is you who are getting old. The stone is only sleeping.

But I caught it, mother, it is mine by conquest, he said.

A stone is nobody's, not even its own. It is you who are conquered; you are minding the prisoner, which is yourself, because you are afraid to go out, she said.

Yes yes, I am afraid, because you have never loved me, he said.

Which is true, because you have always been to me as the stone is to you, she said.

The Ancestral Mousetrap

We are left a mousetrap, baited with cheese. We must not jar it, or our ancestor's gesture and pressure are lost, as the trap springs shut.

He has relinquished his hands to what the earth makes of flesh. Still, here in this mousetrap is caught the thumb print of his pressure.

A mouse would steal this with its death, this still unspent jewel of intent.

In a jewel box it is kept, to keep it from the robber-mouse; even as memory in the skull was kept, to keep it from the robber-worm, who even now is climbing a thief in the window of his eyes.

The Ceremony

With ceremonial regret I lowered a seed into the earth as though I laid it to its final rest . . .

If this seed live again then so shall I.

Which, of course, is sheer nonsense placed in the service of a tongue too long in the damp sleep of its mouth.

From a cloud an ancestor looked out at me. And I thought surely a moment had been reached. And I wasn't wrong, a moment had been reached—and then another—minutes, hours—yes, entire time, before and after me, proceeding in orderly fashion, through me and through the trees like sunlight or a fine rain when the air is so lovely . . .

Had I suddenly become filled with God? Or was it a house falling in upon itself in the distance with a small sigh of dusty desperation? A cloud musty with the smell of old coats . . . The sound of distant calliopes! The trumpeting of elephants!

The Matter

In it were the things a man kept, otherwise they were not in the box: a toy person with an arm missing; also a leg.

Actually, both arms were missing. And, as one leg was missing, so was the other, even the torso and the head.

But, no matter, because in it was another toy person. This one was also missing an arm and one of its legs.

Actually, it had no arms at all; same with the legs, the torso and head.

But, no matter, the box was full of armless and legless toys without torsos or heads.

But again, no matter, because even the box was missing . . . And then even the man . . .

In the end there was only an arrangement of words; and still, no matter . . .

Silence Wager Stories

When I come to view

about steadfastness

Espousal is as ever

Evil never unravels

Memory was and will be

yet mercy flows

Mercies to me and mine

Night rainy my family

in private and family

I know I know short conviction

Have losses then let me see why

To what distance and by what path

I thought you would come away

1

Battered out of Isaiah
Prophets stand gazing
Formed from earth
In sure and certain
What can be thought
Who go down to hell alive
is the theme of this work
I walk its broad shield
Every sign by itself
havoc brood from afar
Letting the slip out
Glorious in faithfulness
Reason never thought saw

2

You already have brine
Reason swept all away
Disciples are fishermen
Go to them for direction
Gospel of law Gospel of shadow
in the vale of behavior
who is the transgressor
Far thought for thought
nearer one to the other
I know and do not know
Non attachment dwell on nothing
Peace be in this house
Only his name and truth

3

Having a great way to go
it struck at my life
how you conformed to dust
I have taken the library
Volumes might be written
ambiguous signs by name
Near nightfall it touches it
Nothing can forbear it
So fierce and so flaring
Sometimes by the seaside
all echoes link as air
Not I cannot tell what
so wanton and so all about

4

Fields have vanished
The Mower his hopes
Bow broke time loose
none but my shadow
she to have lived on
with the wood-siege
nesting in this poem
Departed from the body
at home of the story
I'm free and I'm famished
And so to the Irish
Patrol sentinel ensign
Please feel my arms open

5

The issue of legitimation
Identity of the subject
Circumcision of a heart
driven outside its secret
Elysian solitary imagination
by doubt but not by sight
Fear that forever forever
perfect Charity casts out
The Canticle is an allegory
unchangeable but changeable
Fluttering robes of Covetous
He is incomprehensible he
makes darkness his covert

6

Ages pre-supposed ages
the darkness of life
out of necessity night
being a defense by day
the cause and way to it
From same to the same
These joining together
and having allegiance
Words are an illusion
are vibrations of air
Fabricating senselessness
He has shattered gates
Thrown open to himself

7

Though lost I love
Love unburied lies
No echo newlyfledge
Thought but thought
the moving cause
the execution of it
Only for theft's sake
even though even
perturb the peace
But for the hate of it
questionless limit
unassuaged newlyfledge
A counter-Covenant

8

Mysterious as night itself
All negligently scenery
if Nothing could be seen
Sacraments are mysterious
Ambiguous in literal meaning
the Pentateuch the Angels John
all men form a silent man
who wrote the author down
Sackcloth itself is humility
a word prerogatives array
Language a wood for thought
over the pantomime of thought
Words words night unto night

9

Drift of human mortality
what is the drift of words
Pure thoughts are coupled
Turn your face to what told me
love grazed here at least
mutinous predominant unapparent
What is unseen is eternal
Judgments are a great deep
Confession comes to nought
half to be taken half left
From communion of wrongdoing
doubleness among the nouns
I feed and feed upon names

10

Claim foreign order
dismantling mortal
Begotten possibility
plummet fetter seem
So coldly systems break
Fraught atvantaging
Two tell againstself
Theme theme heart fury
all in mutiny
Troubleless or sadder
Estranged of all strange
Let my soul quell
Give my soul ease

11

Antic prelate treason
I put on haircloth
Clear unutterable
Secret but tell
What diadem bright
Theme theme heart fury
Winged knowledge hush
Billeted near presage
such themes do quell
Claim foreign order
Plummet fetter seem
wild as loveDeath
Two tell against self

12

Strange fear of sleep
am bafflement gone
Bat winged dim dawn
herthe midmost wide
I did this and I
But forever you say
Bafflement nether elegy
herthe otherwise I
Irreconcilable theme
keep silent then
Strange always strange
Estrange that I desire
Keep cover come cover

13

Lies are stirring storms
I listen spheres from far
Whereunder shoreward away
you walked here Protector
unassuaged asunder thought
you walked here Overshadow
I listen spheres of stars
I draw you close ever so
Communion come down and down
Quiet place to stop here
Who knows ever no one knows
to know unlove no forgive

Half thought thought otherwise
loveless and sleepless the sea
Where you are where I would be
half thought thought otherwise
Loveless and sleepless the sea

The Potatoes Have a Word to Say

These are the faces we made down there
to entertain each other. We were green,
marble-sized, scabbed over and rutted
when you threw us into the compost
last fall. After nights of rain that swelled
and softened the earth so we wondered
how any of you anywhere ever thought
it was flat, we returned from exile
and you shoveled us under the rototiller
to be rendered impossible. Fiddleheads
down in the marsh arose from their own
torn parchment and mummy cloth,
and we shoved up, thick-stemmed among
the early unfurlings of squash and beans,
and in evenings of broken thrush music
began drawing gold-centered,
lavender starbursts out of ourselves,
in concert with the sleeping trees:
red dwarfs in the maples, constellated
petals of wild apple. We had toughened up
in that rejects' underworld the chickweed
flourished over. Now you have drawn us
into September, volunteers caught out
in our proletarian jackets, but don't
misread us. Whether as slave food
or aphrodisiac, we have always been
in politics, and though never educated
like the artichoke, or fopped-up
like certain squashes, we can be multiplied
by anyone, prepared more ways than bread.
You are tired of living when you're tired of us.

The Connecticut River in Flood

We were with you, of course,
though for us that America
is over, its energy
siphoned into car phones
going to Hartford.
Still, we can picture you
shoving along on your raft
with the flagpole wrenched
off a neighbor's lawn,

and it looks like
you must have pushed out
across places that never were
until the river found them,
moving at the speed
of old leaves packed deep
as mattresses,
passing water-wimpled trees
on the sunken islands,

dodging snags, watching shad
shoot upcurrent to spawn,
and those Wind River ranges
and Tetons of cloud
whose colors will turn up
in lilacs outside our windows
if Canada dries out, if this rain
ever stops. Even from here
there's a look of imminence
on those bends up ahead,

as though a flatboat might
suddenly happen, with men
dancing and telling lies
for the sheer hell of it,
fleas on a dog, hat slappers,
ring-tailed roarers
and a mouth harp calling the tune.
Or else a pirogue drifting down,
its gunwales barely above the flow,

the cat tethered near the bow
twinned in meditation
with the paddling fur trader.

But who, on our gridlocked bridges,
would hear and agree if you'd yelled
that we're all half-horse,
half-alligator until we deny it?
We were with you
in retrospect, until your raft
ground into this morning's
bullhorns and they booked you
here on page nineteen,
without asking how you happened
onto the roof of Riverpark's new gazebo.

from Wampanoag Traveler

Six foot of mingled orange, tawny,
and black, its underside leaden,
a rattlesnake I kept for study
in an empty rum keg, thinking the vapors
would befuddle him, one morning
lay in wait under that cover when I came
with a snared chipmunk, and struck
my hand, pumping green poison in.

I knew I had only minutes, so cornered
a chicken in the yard, breaking her neck
with a quick upward jerk, and with
the selfsame knife as I had hacked
my murderer to portions, which yet rolled
and snapped along the floor as though
each worked to produce its own head,
I split the hen's belly and plunged
the insulted hand into her still-working
jellies and hot lights, whereon I swear
the thing's feathers wilted and began
dropping away.

That serpent I kicked
piece by piece to the hearthfire, and soon
began a splutter and popping of fats,
a whooshing of steam among the flames,
while on my hand the fowl, now black
as though itself roasted there,
stunk in a way the Devil was in the room.
It too I added to the fire, its vile smoke
offered heavenward, then wrapped the hand
with a plaster.

Along their routes
veins stood and flared to the elbow,
though I plunged the arm in a bucket of
vinegar and waited upon Fate. A tree
tingled and grew from the tips of my
fingers, swelling itself up my forearm
until with a razor I opened my palm
and let my own blood flow.

I rolled and steeped some days upon my bed,
waking at times to discover the arm itself
a mottled snake, its arrowhead buried
and drinking at the chambers of my heart.
In dreams and awake I was rolled in lowly places,
sumps of the deepest hollows, among the pulp
and lichens of tumbled, ancient deadfall,
cobwebbed, prickled with my own drenched bedding.

At times I even seemed to myself a tree,
toes feeling downward toward groundwater,
at my extremities these woody prongs,
scaled, soft-pithed, where juices
wended toward the terminal buds,
which were lapped over and sometimes
in my fevers flowered, blue-lipped,
orange at heart, or rosy and black-veined,
and again like gold-wormed feather dusters.

I was possessed at times with fears and watchings.
Then vermin drew near, their faces large
as my own, lights malefic in their ebony eyes,
each sentient hair distinct, their mouth parts working,
warning against ambulations into their kingdoms.

Some evenings I was settled with cooler moments,
and at dusk, from the swamp and beyond,
a surf of sound arose as from another village
in there. I could pick out some drunkard or
madwoman's denials, but not attach them
to the screech owl, and sounds like someone
hacking brush, and breaths blown across
the mouths of flasks.

I reflected how these
mortal troubles began when I listened almost
from the cradle while the yellow rail sounded,
and a flycatcher whistled, desultory. Later
I stood hours on the threshold of that
bush world, thinking the pygmy owl's bark
a pup crying somewhere, boxing the air
at the end of its tether, and one day
entered a few feet in.

Now at times it seemed
I wandered unattended in landscapes where maroon
leaves of the oak formed metallic masks,
and was observed from thickets by eyes cognizant
of my passage there, and heard such chuckles,
small laughter and rattling, I imagined the mice
dicing, hands pressed on their mouths.

In the few hours of clarity vouchsafed me,
I was capable of depicting the seed vessel of
a lotus, with threatening holes
where the pips were cast, and land snails
nearby, a rubythroat in arrested flight,
grasping a serpentine branch above
a hollowed log whose sockets menaced me.

That bird stares where a green lizard
emerges from a cover of pickerelweed,
engorging a bullfrog by the head, the frog's
feet clawing air. A green miasma ran in me yet.

Another Knowledge

Seven miles from Provincetown, on clear June nights
The summer I learned stars,
Lying on my back beneath the starfields
With my charts and pencil flashlight, learning the way

From the curve of the Big Dipper's handle to Arcturus,
Spica, and then across the sky
To Denebola, the guardians of Polaris,
And The Lyre and The Swan,

I would often close my eyes, resting them awhile,
Taking sips from a can of beer
As I thought of how impossible all this was,
This rented cabin, our summer upon the dunes,

Night after night, the sky like the underside
Of a billowing, glittering parachute
Suspended above us. Sometimes, we'd rise and walk
By the ocean for hours,

My birthsign, Leo, pawing into heaven,
The Northern Cross tipped over on its side,
And try to imagine the feel of Berenice's Hair
And meeting Ettairin in an afterlife

Or spaceship. Would his eye stare so at us?
Would he say, "Get back down there,
You puny things?" Half drunk on modest success,
We hid from the Future

Pretending we didn't care if it destroyed
Or elevated us. In the cabin
A small thin-metal globe the owner's child
Had left or outgrown

Served as a bookend for a small collection
Of Pearl Buck and Taylor Caldwell;
A white piece of driftwood vaguely like a whale
Was nailed to the fireplace wall

And on the screened-in porch
Someone's beginning pieces from a sculpture class,
Not quite bad enough to throw away,
Were not quite displayed. That summer

I'd leave you sleeping to go out
Into the Great Square of the wings of Pegasus,
And climb and climb up through the Milky Way
Alone. I wanted to know

Something I could be sure of, something I could carry
Back to the city, hidden
As tiny explosions of light waves in the brain,
A map I could follow with no end in mind.

On the New Haven Line

This is the day you might have died
And never heard a newsboy's cry again,
Or looked out from the window of your train.
This is the day you might have died.

This is the day news might have flown
By letter, telegraph, or telephone,
To friends from Stony Brook to Riverside.
This is the day you might have died.

This is the day you might decide
To visit Croaton Heights or Sally's Lane.
Because, today, you might have died,
No matter what you lose, you gain.

This is the day you might have died
From natural causes, accident, or suicide:
No more adventures in the great unknown
Of hollyhocks and knucklebone.

This is the day. You might have died
And never seen Rowayton in the rain
Or morning glories bloom in Darien.
This is the day you might have died.

To a Woman Half a World Away

Just about now
you will be dusting the flowers
or changing from your bathrobe into something nice.

The kids will all be out
oiling their bikes, and thinking of birthdays.
The mailman will take his time up the hill.

Maybe this is the morning you will go shopping
to buy a percolator, or a yellow blouse.
Drive, darling, careful.

That book you mean to read
if nothing on the set is well worth watching,
I bet is something with an ending really happy.

Now you are dressed
and walk around the house with your blood pressure up,
looking for something, anything, not in its place.

The mailman comes, and this letter
of course is not there.
You worry just a little as you close the door.

And then you turn, and your face
is just so beautiful it makes me stop
and wonder why I thought I would remember your body.

Here, you will remember, I am in night
beside a river that seems to flow through every field,
learning I am sentimental past my wildest fears.

A Last Memory of Korea

When someone breaks apart
beside you, and you know
he could not swim deep,
and had never touched the *Thresher's* periscope
or filled his lungs
with water where the phosphorescent fish
amazingly sleep
or risked his life
cutting through wires,
explosive, days before
a standing army hit
the coral shore
and you suddenly surface in
the middle of a shopping center lot
so large it does not matter how you park,
around you are the lost Americans
walking toward
buildings, fountains, food,
racks of clothing; at
your elbow is
a lovely salesgirl who
wears fine perfume
and comes from Mississippi. It
was the final days of Panmunjon,
someplace in that little country,
in that measured war.

The Persistence

All the children who were poets
have grown up now,
and up and down the street
they are fixing their houses.

A woman walks her German Shepherd
into the evening;
as if his life depended on it,
a man mows his lawn.

America's great sea of cars
has broken apart,
and come to rest in driveways,
by closed morning glories.

"Why me? And why my life?"
the television asks
a family being assembled
on the living room couch.

Bewildered, the woman goes
back to the kitchen;
under a faucet, she holds
a glass filled with water.

Over and over, she fills it
up to the brim
until she stares at it, pleased
nothing has happened.

Nothing has happened. The crickets
only come out,
the wind only blows. Life only
isn't, then is.

No, that's not right, she thinks,
and remembers a poem
by Kipling—or was it Yeats
who once broke her heart?

Under the hedges, the poets
lie on their backs;
smiling and singing together,
they bring forth the stars.

1970

Urgency drives up
in jeeps of change.

We are heaviness invincible.
We paint our body white heat.
We hang light where the wind does,
and hold cry of pleasure.

Air is anything we breathe or do
to keep alive, or wear to.
Our own pride is as tight as a drum.

We shoot out,
bear guns of accomplishment.
Pigs the color of rocks move
at our touch. The sun
sets all over us, lavishes down.
We are the tolerant winners.
Our words are a nimble chain.
Work is free invention. Time
has no collar.
The only poetry is the release of history
and free use of its hoarded acquisitions.
This is the furnace that the arm, the feeding
hand, goes in, willingly,
in the end,
until the love is annealed.

So let the pact be bound!
Let the love be annealed!
Wipe the bloody foam
from the mouth of morning!

And let even the faintest lapse
of wings, of will, any delay
which is the hiss of time,
pass out of here,

on a skid
out of here.

The Walker

A dishwasher (this morning), an accountant (the hitchhiker
last week), a mail clerk—these are all possible
guises, forms for your life away from us, Henry Faith,
as your story walks on. I have not the final desire to
follow you, an act as decisive to the story-making process
as the suicide's knife. As your story is spun, as the straw
is spun into golden bricks (you were to build a house for her,
in this version relayed to me this morning as we passed
you in the car). She ordered you to build a house for
her, and only then (stamping her glass slipper?) would she marry
you. You did; she didn't. You cracked as glass. In this version.
A dishwasher, a pearl diver, a caster
before swine, if you ask me. You had been a professor
at the university. Animal sciences, my source told me,
my most "authoritative" source (he shared a room with a man who knew
you then), or husbandry, or horticulture. I will check this
afternoon the records I have access to, all the faculty records.
Or will I, and break this strand in the intricately woven story?
Let me sit back and let it spin on, Henry, and on,
as you walk on, in every kind of weather. The evident preposterous-
ness of doing it for one woman, even in those
more romantic times of thirty-five years ago. There is still
the other version. It makes more sense, it appeals to the practical
side of us. Your young wife and daughter were killed in an auto
accident, perhaps even in a car you had been driving. They say
you will accept a ride on occasion, though only from those you
know best (who knows you best?). My wife stopped twice, and both times
you refused her, mildly, gently, distractedly. You nod the same way
when you walk, though you can also direct a nod to friends. You know
people, you sight them on your route and recognize them, you allow
that much contact. Another story is that you are an accountant
at the end of the line in Hartford. You fall off into sums.
The "pack" on your back is from crouching over the ledgers, toiling
with a stub, uncomplaining Bartleby. It is so unlikely
they would tolerate you at the Travelers, traveler, unless
it was because they knew the work they could get from a good draft horse
such as you yourself could raise in that backyard of yours
all overgrown, it needs such trimming a grazing horse could give. Such
least possible interruption of your routines. There must be many of them
at home, inside those doors; as many, and as simple, as the ones we

all know you for. You are famous, Henry Faith, well known
in parts hereabouts. People set their watches by you as they
did Spinoza. Local color, a local character, even pitied.
Every village has its own. I have never heard one person
speak disparagingly of you or call you such a thing as idiot, although
those punks who beat you, cutting through their own highschool fields
to drop you, must have called you such things, and worse. They even
came back a second time, to take your clothes. But the story, the
stories outstrip them. A woman you were devotedly, desperately in love with
stood you up at the altar. Precisely at the altar, fresh in your suit.
(Is it cars, or the women who drive them, that you now shun?) It was
long ago—after the War. The stories grew. The pack on your back,
which is your cares, grew, and the one under your arm
is wrapped in plastic or just a paper bag. You come prepared.
You are a tailor, and that is the day's work, to be mended, to be
minded. Strips of rags. Your day's food. A change of clothes,
as you step into your accounting suit and off the elevator onto
the marble floors of the insurance tower. A mailman (our old mailman
knows you). The pack is letters you have brought home and stayed up
all night sorting. Letters you hoard at home under your floorboards.
Wealth under your floorboards, you wily accountant. Who will you
leave it to? How the world will gasp when they read
of your will in the next day's paper. Will you leave it
to the university where you would have continued to work after you had
gotten married, and enjoyed a certain local prominence, an emeritus, a
pasture? You take the bus into Hartford and get off. The post office
is only around the corner from the terminal, you could work there,
sorting other people's letters all day, musing over the holes under the
strips of light, on a high stool, pigeon-holing. You do take the bus.
That much is certain. The hitchhiker saw you, rode in with you on occasion.
And even though I have yet to take a day off and follow you,
dog your steps like a sleuth, there is time, there must be time
for the story to take effect. You get off, you walk on, your story
walks on. We will swerve when we pass you. We will not interfere.

Gurleyville Road

Gurleyville Road peels apart
as it blends to Wormwood Hill
after rain.
                              In the cleft of the road grows
grass, grows soft and to one side
sloughs off, the soft head of Mansfield pierced
by inessential use.

After the rain the stone gleams: the limits
are not within. The heart

unknits the skull. The air sweeps herself up,
the road also lifts dry
at the edges of my need.
It is travelable this far, won't you come?

The moaning of the meadows, full,
on their shelves along the roads.
The roaring like a sea beyond.
Look out upon hills the color of blue smoke;
send eyes out like doves from the ark.

The Distances

I wait for the frontier
dust to kick up, which is
what dry snow first looks

like in the artificial
glare of the intersection,
the porch of the Hill house

like a saloon's or hotel's,
before I let myself feel
how forlorn the season is,

kicked by wind,
an occasional passing car,
fewer walkers than ever,

each year less, the contraction
without which contrast
is impossible. Such as my friend's

voice from Rome,
all throat, the fullness of a life
in my ear. It is her! It maintains
consistency, identity, after bouncing

off a copper-bound satellite,
and can never fail
to impress, no matter how tired or

mysterious or wise it sounds,
and it does, usually all these
qualities at once,

reconstituted in my ear,
and I am such a young
American again, shorn
of all the intervening time.

First Blood

He didn't know until he'd seen
Troy's towers spiny in the haze,
heard keel striking sand like a javelin,
that he carried the house of the fathers
on his back,
didn't know the weight of it
until he'd swung a short-sword all day
against Hector's lot, arms aching,
thighs spattered with gore,
cheek layed open by a close cut.
That night as he lay shivering awake,
he clung to these images:
the handful of olives he gave the shepherd girl,
the warmth of the Aegean as he swam
toward his father's boat with the wineskin,
the smell of the blossoming groves at home,
the lemons bright in the moonlight.

History Blues

> The waters compassed me about, even to the soul;
> the depth closed me round about, the weeds
> were wrapped about my head. *Jonah 2:5*

Those days
we scarcely bathed off the scent
of one lover before
tangling tongues with the next.
Now we're moving slow and steady
through whatever it is.
It's *mean*, we know that much.
Half the people have got Rottweilers,
the other half
are on leashes themselves.
You tell *me*.
But this day is fine.
Wind has blown away the smog
and somebody is burning sweet wood
in a fireplace.
I don't even mind the plastic Santa
someone stuck
in his front yard crèche, arms thrust out
like Jolson
kneeling before the Christ child.
Could be worse: we could have mortgages
extending into the next life, hearts packed in duckfat.
Instead, we just ripen, give off our sweet funk.
Death knows where I live.
So what. *I don't go to bed with nobody*
don't know who Ho Chi Minh was.
The Zohar
says the storm was Jonah's passion,
the whale his body,
and when he was spat out on the shores of Nineveh
he had the stain of being human,
was worth at least the weight of wet clothes.
Old friend, let's talk about
how our skins have moved on around us
like maps, how our scars
refract the light passing through us as we fade.

The Oracle

On the altar the flies of God
swarm on the pomegranates and roasted oxen.
We say we want to know the truth
but as the light sweetens
and the priestess does not arrive
we grow comfortable with the old lies.
I want and do not want the razor-edged
pendulum that swings in my heart.
The woman gone and why.
Years of wide-eyed blindness.
There is tenderness in all gathered here
in the shade of the temple.
When we were young we dreamed
of a plateau where everything
could be seen in all directions
and suffering evaporated in wisdom.
Silence is the power
that pools in the shadows of words
and when finally we stop speaking
it pins us to the ground

Crows

Hunch in the trees
to gossip
about God and his inexorable
experimenting,
about deer guts and fish so stupid
you could sell them air
and how out in the deserts
there's a dog called coyote
with their mind
but no wings.
Crow with Iroquois hair.
Crow with a wisecrack
for everybody,
Crow with his beak
thrust through a bun,
the paper still clinging.
Then one says something
and they all leave,
complaining
the trees are not
what they used to be.
Crow with oilslick eyes.
Crow with a knife
sheathed in a shark's fin.
Crow
in a midnight blue suit
standing in front of a judge:
Your Honor, I didn't
kill him,
just ate him
and I wasn't impressed.
Crows
clustered in the bruise light
in the bottoms
of dreams.
Crows in the red maple.
Crows keeping disrespect
respectable.
Crows teasing a stalking cat,

lifting off at the last minute,
snow shagging down
from their wings.
Crows darkening the sky,
making fun of the geese
on their way to Florida.
Crows in the roses,
beaks and thorns.
Crows feeding lizards
to their brood.
Crows lifting off road kill,
floating back down
after the car has passed.
Crow with a possum eye
speared on its beak.
Crow with a French fry.
Crows
in the chicken cages
on their way to market,
the farmer
finally gone mad.
Crows hunkered down
rumpling feathers,
announcing the cataract
of snow
over the sun.
The crows prosper.
Carrion is everywhere.
The night
that is coming
is so dark
it will feel
like fur on the eyes.
So dark suddenly
you cannot see the snow.
Thrust your hand in it.
Hear it like sand
blowing on the roof.
A crow shifts his foot
and snow sifts
down from the tree.

Moonflower

Silence wakes me more surely than a scream.
At three in the morning, sound on the baby monitor
is what I listen for: clearing of throat, motor
of hospital bed, flushing of toilet. It's to my father,
to his movement that I am bound. A moonflower,

mouth yawning, arms stretching like petals, he
wakes, slow, sitting on the bed's edge to avoid vertigo.
Sallow skin, the cream yellow of moonflowers
whose stems tighten around their minutes of glory,
their minutes of life, my father curls his fingers

around his cane, his pride. Driving, my mouth
twisted into a handkerchief at a funeral, his death
is what I can't escape. Go to the dentist for a crown,
sure enough, my chair faces tombstones I count
while black plastic bags acrobat the cemetery walk.

Afternoons, asleep in his blue chair, my father
is so still, I stand until I am sure the paper whispers
of lung rise and fall in an eggshell chest. When will I
cover it in tattered shawl of rosebud from Howe Valley?
By the spring, will I be a supplicant by the dogwood

next to my father's grave, my hands palming air
as its white petals do? Bound to movement, there
can be no escape from the rack of this earth for him,
for me, the moonflower, or stigmata on gnarled limbs
of the dogwood that will fall to pinwheel the ground.

Digging Up Peonies

Overcoming fear of stalks that are too close,
I remind myself it's Lexington, that mist

on fields meant rattlesnakes curled in rows
of corn would be cold, sluggish. Like prying

out potatoes with my fingers, I dig up tubers
as if I could lift my father, seeded with cancer,

if only for a day from gravity, from ground.
My parents know what I know—this is the end;

they will not return to this house my father built.
No refugee in Kosovo, wheelbarrowing

his grandmother to safety, I will bring as much
of Kentucky, of their dirt as I can carry with me

on our flight to Connecticut. A bride, moving
to New Haven over thirty years ago, I have

not taken root. I cannot explain this urge
to go to creekstone fences my father stacked,

dig up box after box of peonies I will bank with
Stony Creek granite piled along my side garden

so my father can see pink, fucshia blossoming
from his bed. Is this what revision is, change

of location, spreading, to retell my story
another time, in another soil? Unable to untie

what binds me to Kentucky, to bones of all
those who are in my bones, I will save what

I can of my mother, of my father from this earth,
from the dissolution that binds us after all.

Static Holds a Grudge

So, why do I court electricity, skate my feet
on a shag rug until my fingertips live wire?
I understand why I rub balloons on my head,
stick them to the ceiling. I want to be in demand
as a birthday party guest. Sometimes just to fool

myself into thinking I'm trapped like a lizard
in a jar, I put on a turtleneck. When I'm good
and ready, I stand before the mirror
in a dark room and palm my head. If voltage fizzes
up and out of my hair like carbonation in champagne,

I award myself a Girl Scout badge. Socks fresh
from the dryer don't give me the charge I get
out of running my fingers along the TV screen
to shock my brother and his bulldog. Defusing
them, I come up with a scientific explanation: sketch

polarity and electrons on our blackboard, label static
electricity an impersonal force of nature I
can't control, only work with for a time the way
FDR did two-stepping with Stalin. If I cross
a room, reach to switch off lights, a veil of sparks leaps

out, circling my wrist until my hand is even bluer
than my lips when I dive into the pond out in back
by the livestock barn. Grabbing a fistful of mud
and weeds to anchor me, I stay down as long
as I can. Letting the bottom suck me in until my ears

are a bomb, I toy with exploding, with sleeping forever
bagged in water. Knowing there is surface, I scissor
kick, pull with one arm, spearing through the skin
to air, to light with one hand, the other hanging
onto what blackness can be held from the water's depth.

Number Fifty-two: Winifred Benham, Hartford, Connecticut, October 7, 1697

Joseph, my husband, could not hold his tongue,
said selectmen were no more fit for office than dogs,
threatened to shoot a neighbor who'd named me witch.
Ours was prime land on the east side of Main Street
just south of Center Street in Wallingford. Watching

the surveyor and tax assessor finger pears, spit grape
seeds around my orchard, I knew to train for holy water.
Lowered in a barrel, my life, our six acres would be taken
if I was damned, gnawed by demons that caused me to rise.
Pulled down to blackness, encircled by the hand of God,

three minutes would prove my innocence. My accusers
rehearsed their lines: John Moss, 15, only grandson
of Wallingford's commissioner and Elizabeth Lathrop,
19, daughter of the New London Court judge, testified
I had frequently and sorely afflicted parts of their bodies

too private for inspection. Charges were posted: I read
Shakespeare, not scripture; I appeared as apparitions,
allowing Satan to take my form. Stripped in court,
searched for signs of possession, stretch marks where
the devil must have suckled were found. They matched

a row of spots that appeared while bathing the corpse
of the infant son of Joseph Royce, a founding father
in Wallingford. Other physical evidence was Winifred,
my daughter. At thirteen, she could only be a child
of the devil, being born so late when I was forty-five.

Attending more than thirty trials, I had seen women
who could not sink, struggling upward to surface
for air the rope would suck away. I witnessed women
forgotten a minute too long. Innocent, but hanging
in holy water, no breath of an angel for breeze, dresses

undulated as if to Purcell. I prepared for the judge,
whose brother lived across the street from us, to become
distracted, perhaps by a fit of coughing or a baby teething.
Declared unclean like the cormorant in Deuteronomy,
I learned from gutting the bird how the rounded sea

pebbles in its stomach served as a diver's weight.
Forgetting my skill as seamstress, the judge didn't slit
braiding on my skirt for rocks or prod the oval panels.
I had prepared my answer: bombast, your honor, cotton
stuffing inserted to bulge my dress in Elizabethan fashion.

In bed, I practiced kicking with feet tied, learned how
to count out three minutes, studied where women's
fingers rested when bound to their sides. Burning, lungs
were about to consume me. Pulling the two threads
I had left next to my hands to release slip stitches

binding smooth stones, I kicked to surface, to salvation.
Under holy water, thinking of the judge above me, I found
a darkness I would grow into. Unable to nail my world
back into shape like I did the arbor in my garden the judge
could not confiscate in God's name, I craved a reason,

an explanation to justify my trial. Reading Milton's
description of Satan in *Paradise Lost* who *sat like*
a cormorant in the Tree of Life preparing to work
mischief in the Garden of Eden, I slicked my hair back
like a tulip, used India ink to cover the gray. Deliberate

as Joseph unbuttoning my blouse each night, I wanted
my neighbors to watch me reach up to pluck down stars
as if they were eyes, then bend to uproot ferns with shovels,
sometimes with spoons. Crushing bottles in my hand
to seed the garden, I thought of their swelling nerves, joints

aching as they swiveled while my hatred worked its way
into their hearts. Rubbing my belly while mixing tea, I
added herbs for stomach venom, roots for fever to shake
awake mouths blubbering in sleep. Time surely will
swallow up my place in history as the last witch tried

in Connecticut, but the sight of a cormorant, shining
like a black angel struggling to fly, will keep alive
the cry of a believer fallen. With no final word, unable
to make up one truth to give my daughter a sliver
of comfort, each October, I tell her to imagine God

at an easel, painting leaves sunflower, crimson, ochre,
copper, sienna. Freezing them to edge in crystal, a master
with a trained eye, the artist stands back deciding what
to crop from the canvas, which stand of forest should be
cut and which trees will move to the center of the frame.

A Ripple of Deer,
A Metamorphosis of Bear,
A Metaphor of Mountains

I dream of mountains repeatedly,
running my fingers over maps where they spine
and cluster. Through valleys of rhododendron
and bear, wild pheasant and deer, I near them,
empty and still, leaning over my walking stick,
my breath easing out, a shrill whistle.
At night I stare at stars, cold and still, peaks
of invisible mountains in a sky steeply pitched.
As for crests, moraines and glaciers, icefalls,
seracs, cornices, spurs—they are psalms
of a wild solitude I am brave enough to enter.

In the long journey to be other than I am,
I have struggled and not got far. Each day
I roam the fields, and I climb. I watch
from a shiver of aspen steep on a southern exposure
of cleared field. From the ridge rim of trees—
a ripple. A smooth shade of brown comes to merge
in the fern, gathering stillness and weight,
deer intent on the grass. I envy the deer.
Beyond them, the low mountains unroll. Clear nights,
I measure the cave depths of mountains
and their peaks—then in the hour between night
and dawn, the darkest, I dream into the mountain,

entering slim as a snake through cold soil
and stone. I wriggle down on my back, my soft parts
exposed, falling through caves rank as bear gut,
crooked as roots. *Accept who you are—*
of my labors the most naked and rigorous.
Mornings, I am what merges in the mists as I rise
from these depths, so attached to my ignorance,
I think I'm exalted, more rare than the seven
wise Hindu that ride in the constellation
we call the Great Bear. Then I envy the Bear.

Elegy for a Dancer

She knocks softly,
easing the door shut, the eloquent
bruise along the swell of her cheek
"an athletic injury." Can what she says
be true? I let her lie, I let
us sit there, tangled
in the roots of a vivid lie.

She leafs though her notebook—
I hear the pages tick,
                    still revising
silently my lines about a young girl,
used as a pawn, who sold fruit
outside an officers' club in Saigon,
smiling prettily, until one officer
bent her backward, tore off her clothes
to show that she was wired to explode,
then slit her throat.

Now she shows me her poem,
written about a photograph
that shows in close detail
a woman's dead body,
the men around it busy with autopsy.
She uses a fine word, *firked*,
to say how they take out her guts.
She likens the angle of the woman's
head to her own in the photograph
made just moments after she was born,
her small wet head of dark hair
turned obliquely aside.
She says she wants to write
in the voice of that woman.

By the way she turns in her chair, I know
she wants me to know her, and would
rather I not—she's not a child now.
But I knew her mother,
how she stitched her daughter's underthings
by hand, put by jars of tomatoes,
dilled green beans, spiced peaches.

In charcoal she'd draw for her daughter
the weathered faces she'd known
as a child—Assiniboine—their children's
school, and her own, built on the fill
from piles of uranium tailings
so radioactive the clocks in school
ran funny.
                    Her pain
she painted as thick twists of rope.

I look at her daughter across the desk.
As a child she had eyes of clear amber.
She could imagine, beyond the horizon
of hills gone to rust in the smoke of noon,
our earth borne along on the silken
train of a beautiful woman in a dream no one
has anymore.
                    Her eyes now are smoky topaz,
yellow quartz. She fingers her bruised cheek,
then says softly, as if she isn't saying it at all,
how she has one life openly at school—
at night she's an exotic dancer.

It's not what you think, she says,
but I think *sequins, smoke,*
roving men who tuck money
into her shiny halter, then go outside
with their women, in their heads
a savage tempo.
                    What I can ask, I ask—
my desk and the floor of the office
swept by the tangled shadows
of trees leafing out, leafing through
the window and the scent of beer
and embalming fluids. Then she
eases out the door—
she doesn't want any womanly advice.
She leaves me Vietnam; she has her bruises.
I have this poem, its record of pain at a distance
as a gust of wind thick with lilac crosses
my desk and its litter of books,
bringing with it her voice, without
its mask of nonchalance—
I am your dead daughter.

What I hear is heartfelt, never mind
that I alter the words at their source,
lifting them from a page of raw earth in a book
by chance left open to the wind—
not quite what the Vietnamese prisoner
uttered, so crazed by pain
he couldn't bear to say himself
straight out,
                    desperate, and daring to sustain
beneath camouflage some small dignity
no one can snatch at or plunder.

Icon

I

To raise her spirits
someone has painted her toenails
with a lacquer clear as
the white of an egg but with flecks of glitter added in
to flash like mica,
like quartz in stone.
I have come a long way,
if the common measure of love
is loss, to rub her legs and her callused feet
with a lotion rich in lavender,
remembering how our mother
used to stand at the margin of our room, the door
narrowed open,
and sing into the dark where we lay unready for sleep,
an arbor of phosphorescent stars
pasted to the ceiling.
I don't know if the body believes the words
we offer it, or if it listens
only to the motive below the motive, octaves down—
but I still see her, about to withdraw,
and the stroke of light
that crossed the coverlet as her alto
patience and intimate
refrain lilted over us, like a hand stroking back
damp hair from a feverish forehead.
Side by side
in our twin beds, alone in the dark
our small bodies
already ripening to the sweet danger within us—
to hear our mother sing to us
at the verge of limitless
night, the song offered up from the deep
harbor of her body
must have gathered us, continued and carried us at rest
into the flushed, ready morning.
Ask me now
if I believe in resurrection, body and mind—
I'd have to hum

what little I remember of the song that carried us
all through the night that was
deeper than we could know.
"I've named my left arm Lazarus," she confides,
and I nod,
letting my hands, wiser than I am, work the song
measure by measure into the muscles
of her left arm and leg.
"I see you, " she says, turning her body slowly
toward the side of herself
she neglects, finding me there. *I see you*—said
without surprise or particular
emphasis, as if I hadn't,
all these years, forgetting to remember her,
scorned and disregarded
part of my own heart. When finally I say, "See you
in the morning," she answers quickly,
"I'll be right here."

II

Alone in my own dark room,
I lift my head from hands so wet
with tears they smell like rain
in a field of lavender. Afraid of her life, abandoned and to come,
I flip open my journal
and I see the words
Do not fear. Only believe,
and she shall be well. Only believe.
Credo, it means give your heart, give it scorned and abandoned,
worthy and not worth much,
give it finally, freely.
What seems so far from you, I read,
is most your own.
I take the words into my body. Take them, sister,
into yours. They are light.
Or let me rub them lightly
on your skin, oil of lavender,
oil of rosemary and rue.
Alone in the body's dark nights, in its gardens and hovels,
in its rivers and mountains and many rooms,
together we lie down.

Newspaper Photograph

Beneath a band of broken cloud-light, in silhouette against the morning sky
    a line of women climbs the stone embankment,

a rising line of women, single file, each with a basket balanced on her head—
    migrant women, the caption says

carrying stones in a quarry in India.

They are Bangladeshi—but to my distanced eye they could be figures in a frieze
    on a temple architrave,

or a repeating detail in black slip on a potsherd fired before the fifth century,

women with bowls or vessels on their heads, women with wide, shallow baskets—
    their necks taut and strong, their heads at a tilt

through the centuries carrying oil, carrying wine, carrying the harvest grains
    a civilization depends on.

But these are women in a stone quarry, and the morning mist, I realize,

isn't mist at all, but dust that soils their saris, burns their eyes, silts
    into their ears—they eat dust with each breath

as they climb the rise to spill an offering of stones into the machine at the crest,
    then turn back on the sloped path

to the stone heap, whose rim-line resembles Mount Meru, to refill their baskets.
    And now I see how their coming and going

makes a wheel: a wheel of life and death: a mandala that would interest
    you, Gautam Mukerjee,

wry economist and lover of justice, who once as a child on pilgrimage
    in the mountains above the Ganges

looked steeply up and saw against the brilliant sky a white bird, its wings

outspread as it spiraled into a blaze of light—*a sign*, you said, sent
by the holy man toward whom your journey tended,

the silent voice of the gods made visible—as all such images are: at the least
a caution: a leading: a prayer:

God, make me see.

Skirts

Women spin and dance in skirts, sleep and wake
in them sometimes, ascend and descend stairs.
Some have walked into the sea in skirts,
which is like tossing a skirt over a man's head,
or pressing his face against the tent of one.
Some woman, maybe wearing a velvet skirt,
embraces another woman—so one skirt brushes
against another. Women wash and wring and hang
skirts up to dry, spray them, iron them, hem them,
slip them over slips, over tights. Once, I confess,
I owned six black ones: rayon, wool, gabardine,
linen, cotton, silk. The wind can blow the bulk
of a skirt between a woman's legs, or wrap her in
a twist, billow underneath so skirls of wind touch
faintly, delightfully. Some women hear skirts
murmuring or sighing, conversing with the flesh
they cover. But most skirts drape in silence, the silence
of slow snow falling, or the hushed liquid glide
of a woman's body through a sunlit pool, the sweet
descent to sleep, or passion, or passion's nemesis,
ennui. A woman's spirit lengthens or widens in a skirt,
magnified by cloth and cut and her stride through
the quickened space. If instead a woman wears
a tight skirt, she feels containment and its
amplification—reduction's power to suggest.
Right now my favorite is a crimpy cinnabar silk
I twist into wrinkles to dry. I wear it walking in
the evenings. I vanish as its folds enfold the sky.

The Wooden Egg

I keep it on my writing desk to honor you,
and somewhere you are writing about it,
or rather, about the desire that ascended in you
the day you sought it.

In that town, nowhere decent to buy a gift,
not if you walked across the tarmac
of the parking lot into the glare-searing
mall, not if you drove to that dust-thick
card shop on the square.

Yet your fingers stretched for this made-in-the-
Philippines egg, hand-painted fans of palmettos
and banyan leaves splayed across a deep maroon.
I think you liked the heft and curl of it
cupped in your hand.

We stood on the threshold between two
rooms, May's brash noon light purling
through windows green with trumpet vine,
and beyond the screens, the rhythm of
white clapboard lines.

You proffered it shyly, I remember, and I did
not gaze at you deeply enough to speak
my full thanks, still, for the first time, I felt
your love made tangible in such a silence
as sweeps through snow.

The Banquet

That day, with the lilacs finishing their bloom
and the leaves of newly full trees still bright green,
our table was on the lawn at noon, covered with
white linen, places set, two round vases of blue glass
flouncing the heavy blooms of peonies, the peonies
white and streaked with red. The music of a tenor
saxophone poured out the windows of our house,
our guests not yet come. We were waiting.
You said let's make love now, quickly, while there's
still time. Our bed by the window looked out over
the lawn and the table. High leaves spattered the
table with breeze-shimmering shadows. As we moved,
the silverware and glasses flashed the way the facets
of my ring flash when I roll my hand in sunlight,
so the table seemed to stand for our marriage,
the way my ring does, the long years of our happiness
funneled down from heaven and poured on this
table that stood in the flowering succor of summer light.
We were on the bed and on the table too, moving into
light and into shadow, the feast we had come to earth
to consume, being consumed, both of us host and guest
in easy exchange, our time here a taking and a giving back.

Of Cos Cob in Snow

A December mist lifting from snow, the tree trunks
soaked to umber, splatters, here and there, of russet
beech leaves, lichen grey-green, grey-white snow—
the kind of morning Twachtman liked to paint.
I can step out my door and walk in it, making black
prints of boot in the melt, marking the swizzle lines
of weeping cherry, fan-like sprays of blue spruce.
I crave a Japanese sense of the delicate whole, mad
as a monk for the snowcapped heights of Fujiyama,
the lower mountain suspended in cloud, save for
three storks cutting a diagonal path. A swatch,
a swipe, a drag of the dry brush, impasto next to
the bleed-through weave of linen. An old wall drifts
left and right, dips and rises, wears a ribbon of lacy
ice. How did the painter keep his hands from freezing
as he plodded around Round Hill, worked the easel
into the muck beside Horseneck Brook? Can gloved
hands handle the brush? Americans, it was claimed,
"were formulating an impressionism minus its
violence, force, and 'virile power.'" Well enough.
It's true. Here, in Twachtman, is the pliant, the vague,
the vacuous release, as if the very breath of the year
were expiring in haze, yet how tender it looks, a place
to be lost in and buoyed by, the New England pastoral
the Pilgrims dreamt of. We take it for the save-yourself
virtues of the illumined large in a tonal range that
whispers peace. Cos Cob in snow more than a century
ago, marked by the ever-patient force that waits to move
through us again, caught as the ghost of something else.

Late Autumn Walk

From inside nothing is plausible
But the need for change. Leafing
Through the backcountry's paisley
Ups and downs sways anyone out
For a spin, flamboyants thrilling
The air, a breath of which leaves
One lightheaded with their conceits
Whose bare, forked facts of life
Will be raked against a winter sky.
Or, steaming behind the kitchen window,
To watch a solid week of drizzle
Targeting the pond, tapping out
On oak-leaf clusters monotonous
Ultimatums some have challenged,
Some accept. The wildings drop.
Sumacs flare in spiky disarray.

By November, it all comes clear,
And yesterday's mild invitation
Drew me outdoors— past the pond,
The pasture, into the gully and brake
Whose angry dyes a frost had left
As nutskin, tobacco, cider, plum.
Ankle-deep in that ruined spring,
I faltered over its drypoint details.
Echoes of woodsmoke. Milky pods.
A seed, as if in flight, paddling
Through squinting pools of light
Down the air's deepening current.
One of the maple's thousand hands,
Velveteen cysts tooled on its palm,
Its veins the trace of a character
Meaning both "fall" and "prefer."

An odd momentum kept me going
On toward Sleeping Giant, its easy
Sloping neck and chin stubbled
With pine and birch. I'd climbed
Before—who hasn't?—to the sheer
Rockface lookout they call The Eye,
Known, if by any sense, then a sixth,
For vistas that yield to nothing less
Than blind insight. And yesterday
I stood there like a staff, saw
The whole valley dipped in a cool
Pearl-blurred solution, a glaze over
The gap where the city must have been,
Its edges strewn along a new aura,
The least particular now hovering, not
Settling in the globe I carried home.

The Bookcase

My empty bookcase yawns and rises
from its paint job, white asphalt
newly laid over a grid of back streets,
the chill of what assurance supports it all
still in the air, no music, no voices.
Who wants to live with what he knows?
While I sit on the storage boxes,
my double's slowly making his way
among shop windows and bloody altars,
holding pages to the light, changing
sex to distance himself from force
or faithfulness, the household demons.
It's late. Opportunities are multiplying.
I am what I did? I am what I wait for?
I feel something returning, like a book
put back on the shelf, slid between
names like mine, my story, my fault.

ER

I hesitate to mention now the time
I hesitated—was it weeks or months?—
Before telling him I was leaving, leaving for good,
So that, in the end, it was he who left me,
And my fear of his decision, or no . . . well,
His toneclessly announcing it one night,
Only that, always that, has clouded the scene,
Not unlike the way the years of happiness
Until that day, all of them a delusion,
Had prevented my recalling just how long
I'd waited to discover my feelings at the start.
Two weeks—no, less—on my own, secret cell
Phone calls, a rented post office box,
The desperate joking, the passionate or-elses,
Seemed only to discover the nowhere
I lingered in, the time I wanted to postpone
Hurting myself or him, the time I wanted
To wait until I could turn into something
He would never leave. Years later, forcing me
To divide the shoebox full of snapshots
Or the letters from our long-dead companions,
He waited while I chose, through tears, the things
I didn't want to see, and did not look back
Through the closing door, though it only seemed
As if he were standing there and I was falling
Back, back to a time when I couldn't delay
Any longer, the time I leaned down to select
My lot, lying there on the ground, in the field,
Where I recognized so many others waiting their turn.

~

In Plato's *Republic*, there is an explanation of this.
Twelve days after his death in battle, the body of Er—
Son of Armenius, a hero of legend in far Pamphylia—
As torches were readied, came to life again on his funeral pyre,
And told what he had seen of the other world,
That his soul in a crush of companions had journeyed
To a mysterious place, two openings, it seemed, in the earth
And two others above, between them the seats of judges
Who bound men to their sentences, that they should climb

Or descend, the symbols of their deeds fastened to their backs.
But Er was told only to watch and bear the message back to men.
He saw the dead arrive, dusty with travel, and the souls
Of those already saved step down into a meadow to meet them.
Those who knew one another embraced and wept at tales
Of what they had endured and seen, while those above
Told of delights to come, of injustices reversed, of tyrants
Cast into terrors worse than they had themselves inflicted.
Er then looked up at a column of light to which the chains
Of heaven were attached that held the spindle of Necessity,
Its eight hollowed whorls broadening into spangled ranks
Of wheeling planetary orbits moving as they must,
Each sounding a note in harmony with the rest, and the Fates
Adding their overtones, their hands touching, turning,
Guiding the spindle through its past, its present, its future.
As Er looked on, each mortal soul was asked to choose its genius.
The first were told not to be careless, the last not to despair—
Each would have the lot of his desire, the length of a new life.
Er stood in astonishment as, one after another, men and women,
Because the memory of their previous lives was still so strong,
Asked to be animals in the next, no matter bird or beast,
A blameless, unknowing being not in love with death.
The soul that had once been Orpheus chose the life of a swan,
Not wanting to be born of a woman, hating
The race of women who had murdered him.
Others chose sparrow or horse or, remembering their pain,
An eagle that could circle the slain in their bloody armor,
Slowly circle, high over what men do to themselves.
Then each was given a cup of Unmindfulness
From which some carelessly drank too much
And some too little, so that the past would haunt them.
Er himself was kept from drinking, and how
His body was returned he could never say,
But as the others were driven, like stars shooting,
Up to their births in the world, torches were lit
And Er suddenly woke and found himself
Lying on a pyre, his old parents in tears.

∾

In the end, because I took too long to decide,
The bird-lives on the ground there to choose from
Meant I would have to live far from home.
I chose the farthest, the common tufted warbler,

Native to the Maghreb, a small bird,
The size of a fist, the color of wet sand,
My tail brushed with berrystain, my crest
Opening to the sides its fan of mandarin
Barbules gemmed with black incipient beads,
My call a calling, *er-rand, er-rand, er-rand*.
I can fly to find direction out and sing
Only to attract the echoing air,
But my task, an hour before dawn, is to help
Summon the halfhearted day from its sleep
As the dark begins to tip reluctantly.
My limping chirr, its admonition falling
Into place, glides through the oasis citrus grove,
Switches of scrub beginning to stir and stretch,
To remind who hears it there is work to be done,
Word to be sent ahead of happiness,
Of noon on an iridescent scarab wing,
Of the dank leaf mold and warted rind,
Of the peace in our hours now, for all but them,
Those humans who shout and slash and smell of flesh.
One of them stands alone, every morning, looking
Into water, silently moving his lips. I stay
To keep watch, and something comes back, a sense
From some other life, that because he has never been hurt,
He is impossible to love. For now, he is my errand.

for Edmund White

Churchgoing

after Philip Larkin

The Lutherans sit stolidly in rows;
only their children feel the holy ghost
that makes them jerk and bobble and almost
destroys the pious atmosphere for those
whose reverence bows their backs as if in work.
The congregation sits, or stands to sing,
or chants the dusty creeds automaton.
Their voices drone like engines, on and on,
and they remain untouched by everything;
confession, praise, or likewise, giving thanks.
The organ that they saved years to afford
repeats the Sunday rhythms song by song,
slow lips recite the credo, smother yawns,
and ask for forgiveness for being so bored.

I, too, am wavering on the edge of sleep,
and ask myself again why I have come
to probe the ruins of this dying cult.
I come bearing the cancer of my doubt
as superstitious suffering women come
to touch the magic hem of a saint's robe.

Yet this has served two centuries of men
as more than superstitious cant; they died
believing simply. Women, satisfied
that this was truth, were racked and burned with them
for empty words we moderns merely chant.

We sing a spiritual as the last song,
and we are moved by a peculiar grace
that settles a new aura on the place.
This simple melody, though sung all wrong,
captures exactly what I think is faith.
Were you there when they crucified my Lord?

That slaves should suffer in his agony!
That Christian, slave-owning hypocrisy
nevertheless was by these slaves ignored
as they pitied the poor body of Christ!
Oh, sometimes it causes me to tremble,
That they believe most, who so much have lost.
To be a Christian one must bear a cross.
I think belief is given to the simple
as recompense for what they do not know.

I sit alone, tormented in my heart
by fighting angels, one group black, one white.
The victory is uncertain, but tonight
I'll lie awake again, and try to start
finding the black way back to what we've lost.

Sisters

The school bus drove us home from high school, where
we got off in the Negro neighborhood
and several times a week there was a fight:
one sister called another sister "hoe,"
pulled out black handfuls of her straightened hair,
clawed at her face and hands, and ripped her shirt.
I walked home. I believed in sisterhood.
I still do, after thirty years, although
I'll never understand why several white
sisters walked on me as if I was dirt.
We were all sisters, feminists, I thought,
forgetting what those catfights should have taught.
I was too well brought-up, too middle class
to call a heifer out, and whup her ass.

Juneteenth

With her shiny black-patent sandals
and her Japanese parasol,
and wearing a brand-new Juneteenth dress,
Johnnie's a living doll.

Juneteenth: when the Negro telegraph
reached the last sad slave . . .

It's Boley's second Easter;
the whole town a picnic.
Children run from one church booth
to the next, buying sandwiches,
sweet-potato pie, peach cobbler
with warm, sweaty pennies.

The flame of celebration
ripples like glad news
from one mouth to the next.

These people slipped away
in the middle of the night;
arrived in Boley with nothing
but the rags on their backs.
These carpenters, contractors, cobblers.
These bankers and telephone operators.
These teachers, preachers, and clerks.
These merchants and restaurateurs.
These peanut-growing farmers,
these wives halting the advance of cotton
with flowers in front of their homes.

Johnnie's father tugs one of her plaits,
head-shaking over politics
with the newspaper editor,
who lost his other ear
getting away from a lynch mob.

Psalm

So many cars have driven past me
without a head-on collision.
I started counting them today:
there were a hundred and nine
on the way to the grocery,
a hundred and two on the way back home.
I got my license
when I was seventeen.
I've driven across country
at least twelve times;
I even drive
late Saturday nights.
I shall not want.

Petting Zoo

Spring: the edges and middles
of these roads blossom
with corpses, raccoon, possum, crow-

lunch, bodies bloomed rosy
into meat and gut, colors
saturated. Eye catching

until the eye learns better.
The slow skunk
lingers in brief afterlife

either because the tail sacs
burst on impact
or because it tried

to warn off what was coming.
Pond-turtle crushed to lotus.
Last week the fox flung itself

under my fender—Last week
I hit a fox—Last week my car—
I could make this a poem

about old lovers. I do
worry, slowing down and then
farther down, about being

able to get anywhere.
The thoughtful driver watches
out at all times, maintaining

an easy and natural grip.
I check my fluids weekly,
night after night dream a dim

on-ramp crowded with faint
shapes, fur thick behind
the ears, under my fingers,

my lights, while the back legs jerk
a couple of times. I don't
see for the life of me

how I'd ever end that poem.
My species is all crazy,
think of it, mammals with wheels.

A Walk in Winter

I think it is winter, afternoon.
My father and I walk
in pine woods in jackets
too thin for the wind
and don't talk about the war
we never talk about, the shells,
the minefield he woke in, stumbling
on enemy, the fire he called down
on his position. The needles
mute our steps, our hands
bunch in their pockets.
It must be New Hampshire,
our dark north, though the ocean
of his last home salts the air too
in our mouths. We come out
on a field of husks
waiting for spring
which will make no difference.
We have agreed without
having argued. The ocean is silent,
the trees say hardly anything,
on the far edge birds contend.
Suddenly I'm shouting *Don't you*
understand, I only get one father.
He smiles his hard-worn
comprehensive smile—
some photos remember it.
Then I wake,
a weekend dawn. The day
will wander through its plan,
a few hours' drive
to fetch my son for his night
at my home. I'm getting ready
to hear of his war,
the one someone prepares him
in a room without windows. I too
will figure to uproot my life

to save him from it. He won't know
until the war, the time,
is over. I won't tell him,
and he will have found
his way through with,
from me, nothing.

Tuxedo

(nocturne)

sleek light make black car body open a pool
a pearl
a downtown fool anent sulphur corridor
one avenue dessous that deft umbrageous moon
a half kilo uncut opprobrium
razor dressed
cough up a waiting game simper and hunk mien
a man with a mictive countenance amen
and two legs

tux
tuxedo
eat lux
deluxe

want a flow go easy down past a hi time stream
easy down
korean uzbek mississippi shoe repair and novelty market
down a tendon a brick armpit a high press bridge a bardic white gilt apse of grime
go hotel glass so clean gigantic a car roll in whole
glean class
down block so chock with radio flock it wake cock and shake frock
around you dress-a-rama fancy one video conception
sweet concepcion
mama live in a drum subscribe that dada beat
in a dream go down
way you undawn bundle of city news anon go down

tux
tuxedo
eat lux
deluxe

mister fist twister sit a bumper cop
pose atop fender nose up a goldenest curb this urb presente
hands on a chromous or chromic bastion aghast in a honte night
you tradewar fancyboy and general cream idiom
stand in patent skin for significant american experiment
music suffisant to be felt up earlobe
dotted line endwise suicide under you hood
american experience par none
you cagey grille cut loose a cat lick smilette
hey rat
hey maze master
gambado and falcade curvet and capriole up a countryside
thy flank s'amuse

tux
tuxedo
eat lux
deluxe

quick
identify one right front valve lifter from cylinder five
heat up say eat up say
caseload casserole
he dont know dick about overhead cam
he dont have clem cluelet
he manque a rambunctious perspective
he shine elsewhere if he shine at all
he built on a sandbar
he tilt-a-whirl on a handlebar
he fail bail and trail one aileron
he a main mess all piss and shoelaces
he chevy nova chevy nova chop shop stoolie
you say it
say officer my officer
you bum breath offspeed knave in a blue shoot
say diminutive of test is testicle

hey tux
tuxedo
eat lux
deluxe

quicksilver
give us dog replevin give roach hypothecation
take off this neck brick and wang warrant
make us a morsel parcel
a cummerbundle with no cunctation
a timely lunch apropos that long umbilic road
we sense lex loci and his bandy boys
we riding a line on a shot cuff and a hand sign
mama studs and shirttails
send us to college

Why All Good Music Is Sad

Before I knew that I would die,
I lolled in the cool green twilight
over the reef, the hot sun on my back,
watching the iridescent schools
flick and glide among stone flowers,
and the lacy fans blow back and forth
in the watery winds of the underworld.
I saw the long, bright muscle of a fish
writhing on a spear, spasm and flash,
a music violent and gleaming,
abandoned to its one desire.
The white radiance of Perdido
filtered down through the rocking gloom
so that it was Perdido there too,
in that strange, stroking, half-lit world.
Before I knew that love
would end my willful ignorance of death,
I didn't think there was much
left in me that was virgin, but there was.
That's why all good music is sad.
It makes the sound of the end before the end,
and leaves behind it
the ghost of the part that was sacrificed,
a chord to represent the membrane,
broken only once, that keeps the world away.
That's how the fish became the metaphor:
one lithe and silvery life impaled,
fighting death with its own failing beauty,
thrashing on the apex of its fear.

Art was once my cold solace,
the ice pack I held to love's torn body,
but that was before I lay
as if asleep above the wavering reef,
or saw the barbed spear strike the fish
that seemed for an instant to be
something outside myself, before I knew
that the sea was my bed and the fish was me.

The Paper River

The most beloved body
of my childhood was Johns Brook,
its bed of ancient broken pears,
icy libations pouring
over them for centuries.
Through the leaky oval mask
I entered its alcoves and grand halls,
its precincts of green-brown light,
the light of my infant thinking.
In the minnow-bright roar
I saw the place where life and art
meet under water, stone to stone,
with sunken treasure and trash.
The sound of the brook
was the sound of the house,
the pools of the kitchen and bedrooms.
A galaxy away it would still be
the background of my sleep.

Clouds came down to earth,
great gloomy rooms among the trees,
dark rooms of the brook,
church of deep pools.
As soon as you entered
you were wholly alone in it,
all sinewy ladders
and gray stairs, stones magnified,
and the sidelong trout,
all gone now,
rainbows and brookies,
one big one per pool,
gills like fresh cuts.

I dove into the flume's mystery,
no place you could touch bottom
or see all the way down in
because half at least
was always in shadow.
It was like learning a room
by carrying a candle
corner to corner,
looking for God to see if He, too,
were awake and listening
to the river crumpling and erasing,
enforcing its laws.
I found a cold, an oblique god,
who commanded me to answer
all my questions by myself.

The English language
is also a beautiful river,
full of driftwood and detritus,
bones hung with trinkets,
scant beaches more stones than sand.
And up on the hills it's the wind
touching the juniper spurned
by the cows, its thistle sharpness,
and the fawn's hoof
left by coyotes,
in their scat.

Savin Rock

What I know is a slur of memory,
fantasy, research, pure invention,
crime drama, news, and witnesses
like the girl who liked to get high
and the one who was eventually
returned to her family unharmed.
The rest I made up.

The fathers drank beer in the grandstand,
flattening cans and dropping
the dull coins into the underworld.
It was daylight—we went right under,
down into the slatted dark,
the smell under the bleachers
where lots of men peed,
paper cones and dead balloons,
people jostling and whispering.
Down there were the entrances
to the dark rides, the funhouses:
Death Valley and Laff-in-the-Dark.
Of course that's not true;
they were right on the main boardwalk
under strings of bulbs lit up all night.

Mom says, *To remember something,*
go back to the place where you forgot it.
But the place was torn down
forty years ago; there are motels
there now, where the Ferris wheel
lurched up and over the trees,
over the fathers at their picnic table
close enough to feel the Tilt-A-Whirl's
crude rhythms through the ground.
They make the cars go faster or slower, depending.
After hours the boys loosen up the machines
and take girls for rides.

Hey kid! I flipped a coin in my head
and it came up tails. Want to take a walk?
He looked older than our parents.
How old did our parents look?
He was fifty, or thirty. I remember
the smell of whatever he put on his hair,
and the blue nail on his thumb.
He could flip a lit cigarette around
with his lips so the fire was inside.
I rode a little metal car
into Laff-in-the-Dark to dance
with the skeleton (possibly real
since some teeth had fillings)
that flung itself at me from the dark.

A dog watched me from a pickup window.
The World's Biggest Pig lay
beached on its side, heaving.
The tattooed lady had a tattooed baby.
No one ever tattooed a newborn child
for real, did they? The Chinese Dragon
was only an iguana.
The go-kart man asked me if I wanted
a little on the side. I said no.
His friend in the bleachers
blew me a kiss.
In the Maze of Mirrors
I was fatso and skeleton,
skirt blown up by a fan. Not true.
A fan blew a girl's skirt up.
It wasn't me. I was a tomboy. I wore pants.

At the stable, girls in love with horses
visited and groomed and fed them daily.
For girls it was about trust,
being part of a couple,
the horse and the girl,
but for the man in the barn
it was about making girls feel
groomed and visited.
Come on over here. Didn't a guy ever
brush your hair with a currycomb?
I don't believe it! Not once?

Little honeycomb like you?
And kittens, always good bait.
A little dish of spoiled milk.
Do you think they don't pass them around?
They pass them around.
Marked kids get shared,
little pink kid tongues *lick lick licking*
like a puppy! Good dog!
And on the carousel a man appeared
from nowhere to help her on,
hand palm up on the saddle just as she sat,
squirming there until the horse pulled her away.
Little cowgirl, giddy-up!

Thus she became half human half animal,
and remained so her entire life,
now a shepherdess, now a sleek young
she-goat, so lithe and small-hipped,
half tame, little goatskin haunches—
hand-fed on snow cones and cotton candy—
the girl who was eventually
returned to her family unharmed.

Tell me, little shepherdess,
how this bodes for first love:
the centaur pissing outside your tent
in the afterlife, having come down
over the stony pastures to claim you
and feed you trout and fiddleheads
and take you to bed on the high ledges
where the wind holds you down for him.
But he won't be the first.

Sweet-sharp bouquet of darkroom,
holster with toy six-gun,
hot umbrella lamps nudged into place
by his fat pink fingers.
A little maraschino light presides over
negatives strung up like game to dry.
The tomboy's showing her rump,
hard little buttocks under the tender wrapping,
the skin. Little wonton.

World Trade Center

We are so small beneath the stars
we figure as barely
visible *écriture:*
minute provisoes on the lease
the squinting lawyer can't make out.

Why don't you look at me, you say.

I look but you sit with your back to the window. There
reels the royal document of sky.
Below, in river blackness, a single tug-
boat drags one point of light across the dark.
It wants to punctuate
the entire, shiftless story of the night.
The water, invisible, slides.

We are so small beneath the stars,
we dance, the couples dance, flame fingers air
at each small table from a small glass cup.

We have not been consulted on these laws.

We dance, we look, I can't
read our own sentence,
our candle guttered in its pool of wax.
Outside the stars are wheeling. Bridges string
sequins from nowhere to nowhere. Jeweled words
lie tossed on the blackened scroll:

tossed to the curled, soiled fringes of the world.

Snow

On Easter, snow fell
gently past branches,
joining the old, deep
white, and whether the
ground floated up to
the sky, or the sky
down, who could tell, it
happened so motion-
lessly, all we knew
was suspension in
blankness. Inside,
words fell, gently past
windows, past faces
in front of the windows,
"Why didn't you bring
more logs for the fire?"
"Wash your hands." The trees
stood written on snow,
snow written on trees,
I remembered his face
white, pained, yearning to
speak, and sweat beading.
He did not know then
he would die.
                    Meanwhile,
snow passed into snow,
the family massed
for dinner, the fire
spat, and all that day
I had not been out-
side. I had not yet
entered that white.

Orchard

in memoriam W. K.

Crippled by years of pruning, the apple branch
bends toward me, and I pick
the wizened, fiery fruit you offered years
ago, as you were dying.

Years, it took, for the fact
of your simply not
answering to ripen
within me. Only now

as I sit, pregnant, marooned
in tall grass, cross-hatched
by October sunlight, with the *thunk*
of apples falling, can I taste

your absence. Pale
green, acidic. A spurt
of saliva quickens the mouth.
From the lower field

float yelps and laughter
of children tussling among
hummocks. Their fathers grope
higher into the branches, hands

stretching to grasp
that flecked, streaked
russets and McIntosh. Those men
are woven into a basketwork of boughs

and I am heavy on the ground below
surrounded
by the bruised fruit and a fermenting
glow that rises

as apple haze from the weeds.
You had no children.
But you gave
me a painting of apples

shrivelled and burning,
which I remember now
and again, so that I may
learn, as you did, how

passionately to die. In
time, in time. My child
stirring within me weighs me down.
You have come

to meet us through
the braided seasons, and I see
how, rusting and golden, already
we are following you.

Day Lilies

For six days, full-throated, they praised
the light with speckled tongues and blare
        of silence by the porch stair:
honor guard with blazons and trumpets raised
still heralding the steps of those
        who have not for years walked here
        but who once, pausing, chose

this slope for a throng of lilies:
and hacked with mattock, pitching stones
        and clods aside to tamp dense
clumps of bog-soil for new roots to seize.
So lilies tongued the brassy air
        and cast it back in the sun's
        wide hearing. So, the pair

who planted the bulbs stood and heard
that clarion silence. We've heard it,
        standing here toward sunset
as those gaping, burnished corollas poured
their flourish. But the petals have
        shrivelled, from each crumpled knot
        droops a tangle of rough

notes shrunk to a caul of music.
Extend your palms: you could as well
        cup sunbeams as pour brim-full
again those absent flowers, or touch the quick
arms of those who bent here, trowel in
        hand, and scraped and sifted soil
        held in a bed of stone.

Lost

I am still here between the sun
That rises and the one that sets. To remain
Or go on. Which means to talk,

To remember wind, words for what happened,
How I could no longer figure you
From trees. And a turning of weather so quiet

I grew ashamed. I should have stayed with the horse
Huddled under ledge, but to go back now
Means to come upon myself. To be lost

Is to keep arriving. And so a trail becomes
All trails, perhaps a way out. Which is to say already
I am moving toward voices, each bend of the road

Made worse by knowing what I tell them
Will be different than what I've told myself.

The Harrowing

To enter the field without speaking
Of the bad years is to trust what is

Buried, or at least sleeps. All I bring to dirt
Will rise again through green, what survives

The first plough. Also: an uncertain fawn
Or rabbit taken up and broken by tines

Becomes part of the work, held in morning
Light, thrown to the dog. We mend most everything

Known, marks in a field where we maintain
Others were before, also turning earth

So that one after another we rely on meaning
Nothing, even for what is left behind. In this place, to stay

Only as long as it takes; how to enter
And allow for leaving without getting caught.

The Climb

I will be done with mountains. Let
The subsequent come, the fallen stone.
Let blazes heal, let erosion. Having marked

Certain places, it becomes easier to rest
On the way back down. What name to leave
This flower (or keep nameless), what small rock

To bring back to where I will write you
Of how it was, getting whatever remained
Up to the site we thought highest. The mountain

Does not move; nothing I can say
Will move it. Beyond are only more mountains
Conspiring as if to break free. And I cannot hear

For the noise of breath; each finger uncurls
And one blue flower where trees refuse to live.

Threshold

We got into the room and the room
No longer wanted us. All those dreams
Of arriving suddenly emptied;

The room being all it knows
Of itself, and how we built the room.
What was longing was enough. Inside: the lamp

On the table, cut flowers, done.
Nothing more for us to arrange; you and I standing
With no place else to go. Caught face to face

Until the blink. This, the beginning
Of what the room did. Let the room become
The reason. Let it all be reason, save how

Our eyes move between us, string of
Each end held by the other, taut, quivering.

from Knot

If there's ever identification, that's longing. It mopes, tree-like, rooted yet
Disconsolate. Are birds some of minutes' pockets, or is it natural, this
Bobbing, where leaves release, catching in ignition, thus "spring"? If acts
Graft, each can function as a branch added, permanent in terms of living,
But not. One at most coats or peppers the next, dropping hints, circles,
A figuration. Lets go: dizzy voltage. Where sight recycles, we's glue back in
Place differently, artificial as ever.

In retreat, they're a coil, spark that implodes, will never perhaps open.
The green sucking down into leaves, we jealously sense without touching.
Such concentration inebriates us, even without objects. Consistently
Unspoken, venerating may result in a self, unfocused and blotchy, yet it
Spreads. Then wrap holds belief. Once bandage needs no wounding or
Perhaps the hurt is impulse, one that shies away, harm marks, and you's
Afford no prevention. Somebody turns more numenal, clouded, to envelop
With an improvement on limbs. But where love surges from and is paralyzed
By need, meaning in perhaps every case, does its deformity twist?

"This is one good thing about time, how there's no need for it," says the cat,
Definitive and formless, so American perhaps. Growth, a kind of prayer,
Contradicts hours in a show of dispersal, where what's to be closed in on,
Isolated, is blood, meaning everything invisible, all that composes water,
Each duct. Again, sound. Anyone, in adoration, might wish the air different
As a present to somebody, gentler scarf never pictured or required, a
Mounting so stairs is useless, so the river lifts, so an alarm or all ringing
Trace the most delicate attention, and the atmosphere more clearly folds,
Where privacy's a gift of skin: marking.

Money's from repeatedly asking, which disgusts. So's companionship
Perhaps. To live in iteration or any moment's stream paralyzes and
Silences, where civilized is counting's prime return. Where to pick at
Or worry a fiber, even in conformity or pattern, spoils texture. And phrases
Don't complete because alphabets forge paths; underground corridors.
Where is ambers, which reputedly captures or preserves? In air, so all in all,
There aren't ends to any step's echoes; no bridge back to the bland fizz
Of ice milk, depilatory scents, nodes labeled "home," a voice. Recycling's
That uninflected.

Love says give up and touch immolates. If not, a middle drowns, absent,
Mere, confused, while clarity pledges; threatens on an edge. But "brim,"
As any instrument, body in the abstract, ruminates meaning dreams
Functionally, proceeds by elimination, cut backs, and vacations, sporadic.
The lake, subject to freezing, shows focus but by forgery, not even pools,
Not even tips, not budging. Eats due to abundance; hungers otherwise.
Seethes, the pond. Then a part sets off, a tick, unhinged in the span
Between useless contributions. Chrysanthemums or any feathered bloom,
A draught.

Configurations hollow apprehending by increment, by repetition, which
Overturns momentum, so leaves and ropes pattern and tell no chain; defer
Seasons, flatten days to an option. So disease can detach a route. So cellular
Equal binge or, obversely, gaping. Healing and illness are communal,
Group, stick and fault to every member, swallows. Looming or seeded from
A book or glance, how else could sound make it from one place to the next
As a unit? Except that particles conspire, lodged in each wave, in
Overwhelming homogeneity, so bound. As if all air's wasabi, only mild,
Where stinging's missed.

It fires. Files and fills where we're circuitry, so utterly burned; young.
Thus urban glorifies to crackling. A city, meant as where consciousness
Conserves, based on a compromise, now reduce memory to movement,
When success is in charting, a trajectory, making way, thus wealth. Here,
Judgment's molecular, encoded so rejected. Stained. Flooding thus afloat.
In the thing we're all a part of: nothing or netting, so progressive's
Increasingly participation, so offspring: everyone's bearings herald
Blindness. Urbanity also is prejudice or love, unseeing. The leaders
Set out to locate what they've pictured, with blinkers, thus guilty, heroic.

Here, repetition incites until it ceases. We's play out its minimum
Requirements. Each application coats with some sheen, just as all painting,
Any sense of brush, corrodes. Once in the stream of action you's vanish
In our same midst. Branches redirect breath, so to continue quickly turns
Respiration unnatural. Then to inhale can envelop; umbrella. Discernment
Circles, a waiting that weighs, a prurience, to peel; remorse or remove
Where measure bog down; obscures. They behave, so tailor apprehension
To a politics; swaps existence for iteration.

To clean is a confession. Is all removal archaeology then? And rumination
Scratches. Takes grass as an appliance. Fixes it. When what's uncovered
Is empty, recognition's success. Organs store, thus an impression of abundance,
And everything else takes stock. Bodies are products but in ignorance,
Thinking to act differently, separate, deleted. Even as dust could they mix?
Particles act out adjacencies; impose. What grows sifts and absorbs, recycles,
Trades from the first, dishonorably saturates. There are charts. Exchange
Aims to carry plus consume, where how each accepts indicts all others,
So that possible enjoyment's an offer of blindness, proposition to vacate,
Though laden. The accident welcomes. Because roads come with directions.

from Cheerleader's Guide to the World: Council Book

unsupported catastrophies
hitting the agility exhausted
so fury only's left offense
gravity so rebound cupped
and predictable a loss
still courses still upriver

filled air with spume
as if its equals. A charge
spins in their arteries call

though no words
remain so the storms
in their own minds elude
them and they falter
but receive but gain
yards. The field's

a shore of missing
reservoirs packed crystalline the bleachers

so N0t Righ+ N0w weren't
on the Team and the Team
wanted them. "Come practice with us
here in Twisted or Deceit

Elizabeth Alexander

(1962–)

Tina Green

Small story, hair story, Afro-American story,
only-black-girl-in-my-class story,
pre-adolescence story, black-teacher story.

"Take your hair out," they beg on the playground,
the cool girls, the straight-and-shiny-hair girls,
the girls who can run.
                                        "Take your hair out," they say.
It is Washington hot, we are running, I do,
and it swells, snatches up at the nape, levitates,

woolly universe, knotting, fleece zeppelin, run.
So I do, into school, to the only black teacher
I'll have until college, the only black teacher

I've had to that point, the only black teacher
to teach at that school full of white people
who (tell the truth) I love, the teacher I love,

whose name I love, whose hair I love,
takes me in the teacher's bathroom and wordlessly
fixes my hair, perfectly, wordlessly

fixes my hair into three tight plaits.

Ars Poetica #92: Marcus Garvey on Elocution

Elocution means to speak out.
That is to say, if you have a tale to tell,
tell it and tell it well.

This I was taught.

To speak properly you must have sound and good teeth.
You must have clear nostrils.
Your lungs must be sound.
Never try to make a speech on a hungry stomach.

Don't chew your words but talk them out plainly.
Always see that your clothing is properly arranged before you get on a platform.
You should not make any mistake in pronouncing your words
because that invites amusement for certain people.

To realize I was trained for this,
expected to speak out, to speak well.
To realize, my family believed
I would have words for others.

An untidy leader is always a failure.
A leader's hair should always be well kept.
His teeth must also be in perfect order.
Your shoes and other garments must also be clean.
If you look ragged, people will not trust you.

My father's shoe-shine box:
black Kiwi, cordovan Kiwi,
the cloths, the lambswool brush.

My grandmother's dressing table:
potions for disciplining
anything scraggle or stray.

For goodness sake, always speak out,
said Marcus Garvey,
said my parents,
said my grandparents,
and meant it.

Connecticut

They squint from shore
at scarlet-shirted blackamoors.

The battered boat sails in.
White sky, black sea, black skin,

a low black schooner,
armed black men on deck

in shawls, pantaloons
a Cuban planter's hat—

parched, starved,
dressed in what they found

in the dry goods barrels,
the Africans squint

at trees not their trees,
at shore not their shore.

The *Amistad* Trail

The *Amistad* Trail bus
leaves from the commuter parking lot,
Exit 37 off Highway 84.
There is interest in this tale.

See where the girls lived while waiting
for the boat to sail home, see Cinque's room,
the Farmington church where they learned
to pray to Jesus, Foone's grave.

Good things: eventual justice, John Quincy Adams,
black fighting back, white helping black.
Bad things: the fact of it, price of the ticket,
the footnote, the twist, and the rest—

Done took my blues
Done took my blues and

—the good and the bad of it.
Preach it: learn. Teach it: weep.

Done took my blues.
Done took my blues and gone.
The verse will not resolve.
The blues that do not end.

OH

The beautiful mouth
a flame
again,
shape of such ache
and plenty.
Disastrous intent,

reckon your ascent
in scares and feeble
unforgivings. What's the use of ladders

anyways? Climbing's too far.

The hand doesn't care.
The ear doesn't know.
The leg's done in.

This is the part where you laugh.
Piece it
together and I
promise the tongue will
take it apart.

Wintering the Turn

Because of the snow
        the letter arrives too late.
                "The body doesn't want to know me anymore."

The sentence ends with a comma, and a blue sequined
        lampshade upturned.

Was it how you wondered it would be? Eyesight ascends
        towards what it knows.

What we cannot speak of
        must cover entire villages with ice.

Or was it that you forgot how
        you wanted it said?

Yellowed fingers stretch
        but the shutters remain open.

Inside your mouth
        take the tongue of forgetting—

its familiar alphabet with intimacy grows
        rough and scornful.

Chance narrows into
a crystal champagne glass
and each reflected face
is a blind turn.

Not even a song to offer a way back.

The tracks in the snow
        lead to a wall and a name spelled
                out with charcoal.

What was the word? The world?
        A wound that rhymes with promise.

Annus Mirabilis

One day when there is no breath, thus no longer song
no incantatory, forgiving algebra for the open window
                    and the wind,
                              and the wasps stirring along the sill
                              in late March.

                              Not cinder, not smoke, and what all
                              else that will

                    not be there. No more.
Is it enough, then to glimpse another's
reflection in a picture window backed by night,
lit by Chilean wine and soft voices?
          The melon's syrup slicks someone's
cheek; a napkin thick with the scent
                    of currants and folded in thirds
          falls to the floor.

Outside, the lawn furniture levitates above
          the sleepy eyes of mute animals led astray.
No other world but this. This.

Mise En Scene

Say
it is winter, and through the snow
a dark figure—a man—crosses
a bridge between you and there. Say
he stumbles back,
his pink tongue uncurls like a comma as he calls your name,
                                        any name as he falls, that is if
he does, over the side, his scarf spread
above him like an upper lip, narrowing
against   the winter   sky.

How would you begin to describe
it with words hollowed out by sound?

And how does this occur to you later,
                              recur as syllables

and each vowel offers the place where you'd want
to invent a new opening
but there is no new place that lies
        fallow, unburdened
                              by appearance.

Instead you repeat to yourself: *The paddock door*
is unlatched or
        the burner
of the gas stove
        is wide open
and anxiety sets the world in motion:
                                        an incantation for the universe
stretched taut like the brim of a bowler hat

into which Houdini pours
a pitcher of bourbon.

But memory is pixallated,
flickers horizontally and
                    (did you try
the vertical

hold?) the screen grows hazy
like the cigarette smoke darkening Rod Serling's
Botany 500 suit on a plastic black and white TV set.

Indirection as a means of accounting—the scarf
was red, his boots
untied,
but yes you see still he did fall—and his fingers
splayed apart—as if the right details could quarry
the moment before our eyes
but the truth
is you can't really say
what belongs, can you?

So invent a plot by which he is brought
to the edge of the bridge, which gives the authority
for the figure to slip.

Wait, did you make the whole thing up?
(It'd be so much easier if it made sense.)

Telling gathers, whatever its worth, the ordinary
and how we are fashioned—bewildered

by a language in which nothing appears or
disappears, but draws
closer in—as the hushed crowd
circles Houdini and his empty sleeves.

Think of a mirror would you as a shoring up of trust
as a place to start, a place to agree

sequins
spin and wobble across the bedroom floor

yessing this moment into the next—
(sequence)

What happened next? The reflection does not hold.
The facts interrogate the space of a moment

while you
woke and fell over woke and fell over
the terror of partial knowledge

only to begin
to begin again.

Now a quarter whirls and clatters along
a tabletop collage of broken glass and coral.

But don't forget too the snow
and the bridge
and the man

who fell, not falls, and that
never
changed.

The Death of Towns

> We have been in effect, conducting a vast toxicological experiment,
> and children are serving as laboratory subjects.
> *—Dr. Philip Landrigan, former special advisor to the*
> *Office of Children's Health Protection of the* EPA

I remember I thought it was a church.
When I was young I thought the factory
was a church because it rose
from the hills and breathed.
But mostly because my father left home,
walked through the gates, head bent,
and prayed there and was cast out,
bleary eyed, huddled and wheezing.
And because the waters shone, glistened
at night, and the fish we found on the shores of the
bell-works were boneless, immaculate.

Because it hurt when he came
out I thought he was wholly
well. Then silence and not
a cry so much as the bell
grasped mid-swing, an "o"
starting as it stops.
I was alone and heard
him breathing, asked
"What" and "How."
And I looked and was afraid.

You never saw one alive.
They just littered the shore,
fist-sized, finless, no real shape.
You'd wonder how they lived so long,
got so big. Some didn't have eyes
and others wore their organs
on the outside, bee-sized heart
peeking through and once a tongue
like a lick of hair. They were still
there after they shut the bell-works down,
after the waters started to clear.

Because he was boneless, lolling.
Because stumps for arms.
Because eyeless, empty plane
from forehead to perfectly formed
nose. Because glistening
mouth, mucus, a pane cloaking the "o,"
every window I'd ever turned from.
Because he was a fish
they said I shouldn't feed him.
Should leave him, try again.

Sometimes I would take her there
and we would lie beside the shore.
That first time she bled and cried
a bit. I told her about bells,
how it took twelve men to lift one.
I didn't say my father saw a man fall
into the cast when the bronze was
being poured. How his screams
came back to him, how you could
feel them in the floor. She said,
The water shines like bells.

They said starving takes time
so I shouldn't stay. But I could
hear him everywhere, the wish
of his breath, the way it echoed
in the bell of him as though he was filled
to bursting with horses
sighing and chafing against
each other. His father looked
at him and reared up.
And his sweat was like weeping.

The first time I saw him
I thought of my father coming
home burned and gasping for breath.
How at the end of his life, after
the factory closed, he shuddered,
troubling the surface, his mouth
grasping for any small thing. He'd say,
The snow is so red and Who is that
screaming? He'd say, *Oh God*
it's in the water. He'd say, *My God*
we dumped it in the water.

Flutter. The flutter of his chest.
Breath. Birds perched restless on his gums.
The nurses came in. They'd bathe him.
It made me want to laugh,
their need to keep him clean.
As if he could even soil himself.
As if there was anything but air inside.
Heart. Somewhere a thimble-sized drum.
Arms. No arms but reaching.
In a dream I named him Hunger.

It took awhile to shut it down.
First the machines stopped,
their heaving slowed to a shy wheeze,
then lights turned off, floors swept,
the massive bones of bells left naked
behind doors and finally the heat
receding, lonely caverns cooling one
by one until the last man made his way
out the door, hand working
the back of his neck, back and forth
through the night.

It takes three days to starve a child,
to convince the stubborn drummer
it's time to go home. He struggled.
He arched his back as though pulled
by a current and would not cool.
His tongue licked at the air
and he wept though his silence
was worse and held us
like beasts who are no lighter
for having been bled.

Late Twentieth Century in the Form of Litany

The winter continued and I thought I heard voices.
Butchers sharpened their knives and I thought I heard voices.
Roy Orbison moaned and I thought I heard voices.

In the dark room of childhood I thought I heard voices.
My bike chain came loose and I thought I heard voices.
Mother choked on the bit and I thought I heard voices.

A war raged outside and I thought I heard voices.
My saxophone gleamed and I thought I heard voices.
The drive-in went dark and I thought I heard voices.

The speakers kept sizzling and I thought I heard voices.
Boys came in the pews and I thought I heard voices.
Mother choked on the bit and I thought I heard voices.

The mills locked their doors and I thought I heard voices.
Elvis kept playing dead and I thought I heard voices.
I watched her undress and I thought I heard voices.

Boys lit cats on fire and I thought I heard voices.
Flames crept toward our yard and I thought I heard voices.
The Klan marched through town and I thought I heard voices.

I met my maker and I thought I heard voices.
Gas filled the garage and I thought I heard voices.
I lied at confession and said I heard voices.

Someone shot J.R. and I thought I heard voices.
She said, "Get me out" and I thought I heard voices.
My vision got worse and I thought I heard voices.

I crawled into bed and I thought I heard voices.
The highway came through and I thought I heard voices.
I met my maker and I thought I heard voices.

I danced in my bedroom and I thought I heard voices.
The curtains caught fire and I thought I heard voices.
Mother took all the pills and I looked at the clock.

I placed my hand on the turntable and I thought I heard voices.
Joan Jett sang "Crimson and Clover" and I thought I heard voices:
Over and over I thought I heard voices.

Final Note

The comments, anecdotes, facts, and tidbits below are meant to enhance a reader's experience of these poems without becoming intrusive. These annotations are far from exhaustive. They do not identify every reference, but rather provide some links between the poems or poets to things particularly Connecticut.

For example, Joel Barlow wrote his popular "Hasty Pudding" poem to assuage homesickness while engaged in diplomatic work in Savoy. The local landscape reminded him of Connecticut, and when the inn where he stayed served a cornmeal dish, memories overwhelmed Barlow: the famous poem followed almost spontaneously. Nonetheless, Barlow believed it inferior to his nationalistic epic poems, such as *The Columbiad*. Patriotic poetry typifies the writing of Trumbull, Dwight, and Humphreys, as well as Barlow. While Trumbull's *Progress of Dulness* satirizes aspects of contemporary educational practices, *M'Fingal* meant to stir readers' emotions in the interest of independence. Dwight's *Greenfield Hill* depicts and praises the character of Connecticut's people, institutions, and landscape. And Humphreys's *Address* sought to offer encouragement and inspiration to the American troops. The brief excerpt from Barlow's *Columbiad* provides a short review of Trumbull, Dwight, and Humphreys as American nationalistic and patriotic voices. James Abraham Hillhouse dedicated his apocalyptic poem *The Judgment* to John Trumbull, and the excerpt from *Sachem's Wood* included here describes a view from West Rock, New Haven. The poems of Hillhouse, Sigourney, and Stowe, though they evoke the past, turn toward moralistic instead of nationalistic themes.

With Brownell, Gilman, and Branch, the poems in this anthology begin to take on a modern timbre. Henry Howard Brownell may use a Latin title—"Suspiria Ensis," which literally means "sighs of the sword" or, more poetically, "sorrow of the sword" or simply "war laments"—but this poem written aboard Farragut's ship, the *Hartford*, evokes the horrors of war by noting the suffering that occurs on both sides of a battle. Charlotte Perkins Gilman's poem of advice, "To the Young Wife," which questions the "wooden palace and yard-fenced land," anticipates the angst of suburban women of the post–World War II era. Anna Hempstead Branch's "Connecticut Road Song" incorporates the names of quite a few of the state's towns. These designations she places alongside biblical place names. In the play here between the contemporary and the timeless, transience wins, for the traveler must move ever on to the next location.

Wallace Stevens's poems herein are also full of Connecticut places and place names: Haddam and Hartford, the pond at Elizabeth Park, and the church steeple in Farmington. But as in Branch's "Connecticut Road Song," Stevens uses the familiar to make extraordinary statements about or explore complex ideas. The writer-scholar Ronald Sukenick once said, regarding "An Ordinary Evening in New Haven": "A summary of the poem would be of small help, since there is no argument to the poem, nor progression of any kind." Stevens himself said of this poem that its goal is "to try to get as close to the ordinary, the commonplace, and the ugly as it is possible for a poet to get." Various permutations of the imagination and reality may be Stevens's theme, and so in "The River of Rivers in Connecticut," no particular river is the object or the subject of the poem but rather that river "this side of Stygia," this side of non-existence.

Charles Olson wrote his early poem "Variations" for a young art student at Black Mountain College in North Carolina; more significant than its dedication is how the poem echoes the work of the northeasterners William Carlos Williams and Wallace Stevens, and draws directly from a poem by Arthur Rimbaud. James Laughlin wrote his long poem *Byways* late in his career but early in the pre-dawn hours at his Norfolk, Connecticut, home, Meadow House.

William Meredith's "The Wreck of the Thresher" recalls the loss in deep-sea-diving tests of a nuclear-powered submarine some two hundred miles east of Cape Cod. Portsmouth Naval Shipyard built the *Thresher*. If Meredith's poem has its origin in harsh reality, James Merrill's excerpt from *Mirabell* has its origin in a magical playfulness that is as much highly wrought philosophical intellectualism as is Stevens's "Ordinary Evening." *Mirabell: Books of Number* is one book-length section of Merrill's monumental epic poem, *The Changing Light at Sandover*. In this work, Merrill and David Jackson use a Ouija board not only to communicate with spirits of the deceased but to be guided through various realms of history, legend, and science. Through much of this book, Mirabell, a fallen angel, describes an attempt at the creation of an earthly paradise. Listening are Merrill, Jackson, their deceased friend Maria Demertzi Mitsotaki, and the deceased poet W. H. Auden. The excerpt herein refers to Stonington, Connecticut, and the Merrill-Jackson home on Water Street, where the lessons from Mirabell unfold.

F. D. Reeve recalls that he wrote "Night River" while "watching the Connecticut one evening at Essex [. . .] and remembering children playing on the Hudson docks in New York City." He wrote "Identity Crisis" "thinking of college students (Wesleyan) in the 60s," while "Watersong" came out of the experience of fly-fishing on the Housatonic River.

Lewis Turco's "The Recurring Dream" is about his father, minister of the Italian Baptist Church of Meriden. Gaetano Lisi converted the immigrant Luigi Turco to Baptism in Wakefield, Rhode Island. After becoming a minister, Luigi served congregations in Buffalo and Meriden. In the latter city, the Italian Baptist Church eventually became the Grace Baptist Church.

Susan Howe wrote her profoundly spiritual poem "Silence Wager Stories" "in Guilford [. . .] during the summer and," she wrote, "it has the spirit of the Connecticut landscape by Long Island sound where I live in it."

Brendan Galvin's *Wampanoag Traveler* is a book-length poem based on Loranzo Newcomb, a natural historian of early eighteenth-century New England. Galvin used surviving correspondence for the composition of his poem.

"Like so many others," Dick Allen has said, "I often take the New Haven line down to New York City." In his poem "On the New Haven Line," the clause "This is the day you might have died" repeats several times. According to Allen the line "had entered my mind one day when I was on the train, and it stayed there for several years until the poem's form found it."

George F. Butterick's poem "The Walker" recalls a University of Connecticut local legend, while "Gurleyville Road" depicts a main thoroughfare in Storrs, Connecticut, that runs from the campus down to the Fenton River. A different sort of road poem is Doug Anderson's "Crows," which mentions "Crows lifting off road kill, / floating back down / after the car has passed." Anderson wrote the first draft of this poem while "sitting in a diner in Middletown contemplating crows visiting road kill." J. D. McClatchy's "Late Autumn Walk" takes place off-road in Sleeping Giant State Park.

Margaret Gibson wrote "Elegy for a Dancer" while she was a poet-in-residence at the University of Connecticut. "The young woman in the poem," Gibson writes, "was in my creative writing class, someone who, as the poem relates, I'd known since she was a very young girl."

Gray Jacobik associates her poem "Skirts" with Pomfret, Connecticut, because she lived there when she wrote it and often went for evening walks, although, as she says, "rarely in a skirt." More directly Connecticut-inspired is Jacobik's "Of Cos Cob in Snow," with its reference to John Henry Twachtman (1853–1902), an American impressionist. After studying in Paris, Twachtman moved to Greenwich, Connecticut, in 1886. He painted and exhibited with J. Alden Weir and spent considerable time at the artists' colony in Cos Cob, Connecticut.

Chase Twichell notes that "Savin Rock was an amusement park on the Connecticut coast not far from New Haven, where I grew up. In the late nineteenth century it was a glamorous place, but by the 1950s it had more of a sleazy carnival atmosphere."

Elizabeth Alexander's poem "The *Amistad* Trail" refers to that major event in Connecticut and United States history: the 1839 seizure of the ship *Amistad* by fifty-three illegally "purchased" Africans. An American brig intercepted the *Amistad* off Long Island, and the Spaniards who had enslaved the Africans were freed while the Africans were imprisoned on charges of murdering two Spanish sailors during the takeover aboard the ship. President Martin Van Buren wanted the Africans extradited to Cuba, but abolitionists and others sought a trial in America. A hearing in Hartford initially freed the Africans, but the case continued on appeal all the way to the Supreme Court, where, defended by former president John Quincy Adams, the Africans were finally recognized as free men.

In post–World War II New England, "the death of towns," as Gabriel Calvocoressi titles the penultimate poem in this collection, occurred frequently. In Calvocoressi's hometown of Meriden, Connecticut—once known as Silver City because of the products manufactured there—the old factories closed and left unemployment and environmental destruction behind. For example, Bradley and Hubbard Manufacturing Company began in 1852 and in 1940 became part of another local manufacturing firm, the Charles Parker Company. In the 1940s the company made materials for the war effort, but in the 1950s business declined and then disappeared altogether. Union Manufacturing Company of New Britain, Connecticut, bought Parker in 1957, and in 1976 a spectacular fire destroyed all the abandoned buildings of the long-closed Bradley and Hubbard Manufacturing Company.

About the Poets

ELIZABETH ALEXANDER achieved international fame when she recited her poem "Praise Song for the Day" during the presidential inauguration ceremony for Barack Obama on January 20, 2009. Alexander received her bachelor's degree at Yale University and is currently professor of African American Studies at Yale. The author of seven collections of poetry and two collections of essays, her first collection of poems for young adults, co-written with Marilyn Nelson, *Miss Crandall's School for Young Ladies and Little Misses of Color,* received a 2008 Connecticut Book Award. Alexander lives in New Haven, Connecticut.

DICK ALLEN's seventh poetry collection, *Present Vanishing*, received the 2009 Connecticut Book Award in poetry. He has also received the Hart Crane Poetry Prize, and in 2010 he became Connecticut's poet laureate. Allen was the Charles A. Dana Professor of English and the director of creative writing at the University of Bridgeport, where he taught from 1968 to 2001. In the 1970s and '80s, Allen became a key figure in the expansive poetry movement that broadened poetry beyond concerns solely of the self and that advocated the use of traditional poetic forms. Allen told a *Hartford Courant* reporter: "The best poetry is like an iceberg. You can see part of it on the surface. I hope my poetry has a little, a third, above the surface."

DOUG ANDERSON's first book of poetry, *The Moon Reflected Fire*, received the Kate Tufts Discovery Award for poetry. Anderson is a Vietnam War veteran, and he has published fiction, film scripts, reviews, and criticism. Recently he published his powerful and poetic memoir *Keep Your Head Down: Vietnam, the Sixties, and a Journey of Self-Discovery.* Anderson lived in Hartford, Connecticut, for many years, and he has taught creative writing at the University of Connecticut Hartford campus and nonfiction writing in the low-residency MFA program at the Pacific University of Oregon. He currently resides in Northampton, Massachusetts.

JOEL BARLOW, the son of a Reading, Connecticut, farmer, lived an extraordinary life. After a brief time at Dartmouth College, he returned to his home state and entered Yale. As the Revolutionary War had begun, Rev. Charles W. Everest wrote, "while [Barlow] still applied himself during the sessions of college faithfully to his classical pursuits, he employed his vacations in fighting the battles of freedom." Following in the footsteps of Timothy Dwight, Barlow became an army chaplain, but at the cessation of hostilities he turned toward the law. He had already begun his career as a poet, having completed "The Vision of Columbus" while in the army. He moved to Hartford where he became one of the Hartford Wits, edited a weekly gazette called *The American Mercury*, and for a short time owned a bookstore. He went to France first on a business venture and wrote poems and essays on contemporary events, as well as his popular poem *The Hasty Pudding.* In 1795 President Washington appointed Barlow consul to Algiers, where he secured the release of American captives there and in Tripoli and Tunis. He made a sizable fortune in France through commercial speculation and, after seventeen years away, returned to the United States, settling in Washington, D.C., in a stately house he called "Kalorama." In 1808 the final version of his epic *The Columbiad* was published. In 1811 President Madison appointed Barlow minister plenipotentiary to the court of France. Near the end of the following year Barlow died in a small village outside Cracow, Poland, while enroute to meet the Emperor Napoleon.

ANNA HEMPSTEAD BRANCH was born in Hempstead House, New London, Connecticut, one of the oldest and best-documented houses in New England. She would also die there in 1937. Her mother wrote popular children's books and poems, and her father was a New York lawyer. Branch graduated from Smith College in 1897, then studied dramaturgy at the American Academy of Dramatic Arts in New York. She divided her time between Hempstead House and Christodora House, a Lower East Side settlement house in New York. At Christodora she founded and organized the activities of the Poet's Guild. The guild brought poetry to the neighborhood, but also served as a reading and discussion venue for poets such as Edwin Arlington Robinson, Vachel Lindsay, Sara Teasdale, and Carl Sandburg. Robinson considered Branch a major poet of the day. Her career began with a flourish when she won first prize for a poem by a college graduate in a contest sponsored by the *Century Magazine* in 1898. Her first book, *The Heart of the Road*, appeared in 1901. *Last Poems*, published seven years after her death, was edited by the well-known poet Ridgely Torrence. Her papers are in the Rare Book Room at Smith College and in addition to drafts of poems contain correspondence with notable writers of her day, such as William Rose Benet, Lindsay, and Robinson. After her death Hempstead House became part of the Connecticut Landmarks historical and preservation organization. The house is open for tours from Memorial Day through Columbus Day.

HENRY HOWARD BROWNELL was born in Providence, Rhode Island. His father, a physician, moved the family to East Hartford, Connecticut, four years after the poet's birth. Brownell graduated from Trinity College, then called Washington College, in 1841. In 1844 he completed his study of the law and was admitted to the bar. In 1851 he published the *People's Book of Ancient and Modern History.* He achieved his highest recognition for the composition of war poems, especially regarding naval battles. Oliver Wendell Holmes called Brownell "Our Battle Laureate." In his introduction to Brownell's *Lines of Battle and Other Poems* (1912), M. A. De Wolfe Howe (Susan Howe's grandfather), quotes a private letter of Dr. Holmes written years after the poet's early death in 1872: "Mr. Henry H. Brownell was one of the most gifted men I have ever met. The grasp of his mind, the vigor of his imagination, the strength of his memory, and the way in which he used it in conversation, all made him a man to be remembered." Admiral Farragut appointed Brownell his secretary aboard the *Hartford* during the Civil War, and the eyewitness battle poems that resulted brought the poet esteem and recognition. After the war he returned to East Hartford where he died in his early fifties. As Howe notes: "His disease was cancer of the face, and for the quiet courage with which he endured his pains it is enough to say that on one occasion he insisted upon watching the surgeon's operation upon him, by means of a mirror which he held in his own hand."

GEORGE F. BUTTERICK was a poet-scholar-editor-archivist-professor at the University of Connecticut before his untimely death at the age of forty-five due to cancer. Previously published in six short collections, *The Collected Poems* (1988) offers a rich variety of poetic expression. Butterick's work shows a facility with everyday and idiomatic language, a sense of humor, and lines, like Thoreau's, that are memorable individually ("the leg of these times gimps forward"). There is also, understandably, the presence of Charles Olson in his work. In his time, Butterick edited *Charles Olson and Robert Creeley: The Complete Correspondence*, co-edited with Donald Allen *The Postmoderns: The New American Poetry Revised*, and published the more than eight-hundred-page-long *A Guide to* THE MAXIMUS POEMS *of Charles Olson*. This work not only helped popularize Olson but also set the standard for editorial work on poetry. Susan Howe has said that Butterick's "editing of Olson has to be one of the most generous gifts to poetry in my time. Priceless. [. . .] The fractured syntax, the gaps, the silences are equal to sounds in *Maximus*. That's what Butterick saw so clearly. He printed Olson's Space." Butterick was the curator of literary archives at the University of Connecticut, and he received an American Book Award for editing the *Collected Poems of Charles Olson*.

SOPHIE CABOT BLACK lives on the same small farm where she grew up in southwestern Connecticut. She teaches at Columbia University, where she received her MFA degree. Her first book, *The Misunderstanding of Nature*, received the Norma Farber First Book Award and her second book, *The Descent*, received a Connecticut Book Award. She began writing poems after a public school teacher inspired her with a writing exercise, and she spent a lot of her childhood in the local library after school, reading whatever she could get her hands on. Beside the landscape of Connecticut, time spent in Colorado and in Maine has also influenced the tone of her work. *The Los Angeles Times Book Review* has called her voice "startling, jagged and implacable" and noted that "*The Descent* is steep, precipitous and dazzling—all the way down from a hard-earned heaven."

GABRIELLE CALVOCORESSI grew up in Meriden, Connecticut. Her first book, *The Last Time I Saw Amelia Earhart*, received the 2006 Connecticut Book Award in Poetry. Her poems of direct evocative language make masterful use of internal rhymes, ironic juxtapositions, haunting sounds, and images. Her poems are accessible, but they are also inventive adventures in language—precise in thought, compelling in emotional force, and diverse in form. Both of her books contain poem sequences. *Apocalyptic Swing*, her second book, contains a seven-poem sequence, "Training Camp: Deer Lake, PA," that examines the intersection of faith and sport in contemporary America. Another sequence, "Circus Fire, 1944," included in her first collection, recalls a tragic event in Connecticut history. Calvocoressi said in an interview, "The poem (to me) is a contract as much as anything else. That means we both have a responsibility in our engagement with it." She now resides in Los Angeles and teaches in the graduate writing programs of California College of the Arts and Warren Wilson College.

HAYDEN CARRUTH was born in Waterbury, Connecticut. During his lifetime he published more than thirty books, edited *Poetry* magazine for a brief time, and served as poetry editor of *Harper's*. He edited a number of anthologies, including the inexpensive paperback that introduced many future poets to the art during the 1970s, *The Voice That Is Great Within Us: American Poetry of the Twentieth Century*. For his poetry he received a Pulitzer Prize, a National Book Award, and a National Book Critics Circle Award, among many others awards and honors. He was a close friend of James Laughlin's and wrote his *Norfolk Poems* (1962) while staying at Laughlin's rural Connecticut estate. Carruth also published a memoir about Laughlin, *Beside the Shadblow Tree* (1999). Carruth's poems could be written in traditional forms or jazzlike improvisations. He told *Contemporary Authors*: "My poems, I think, exist in a state of tension between the love of natural beauty and the fear of natural meaninglessness or absurdity."

RICHARD DEMING, a resident of New Haven and a lecturer at Yale University, is a poet and a theorist who studies the philosophy of literature. He is coordinator of the Yale Contemporary Poetics Group and the author of *Let's Not Call It Consequence*, winner of the 2009 Norma Farber First Book Award from the Poetry Society of America. He is also the author of *Listening on All Sides: Toward an Emersonian Ethics of Reading*. Deming is currently writing a study of the ordinary in modern and contemporary poetry. With Nancy Kuhl, he runs Phylum Press, a small, independent poetry publisher. Deming said in a profile published in the New Haven *Arts Paper*: "If we say a poem resists easy summation, easy reading, and then we have to give more of ourselves—at least our time—to respond to it, then we're discovering ourselves through that act."

STACY DORIS was born in Bridgeport, Connecticut. Her first publications of poetry, at ages six and seven, were in a journal published by the Fairfield Public Library for their young poets series. She received her undergraduate degree in literature from Brown University and an MFA in English and creative writing from the University of Iowa. She translated contemporary French writing into

English and contemporary American writing into French. She worked in collaboration with visual artists on book projects. About Doris's work *Paramour,* the poet Sianne Ngai said, "A box of prosodic bonbons with exploding centers, offering the burst of intensity only artificial flavors can provide." For several years, Doris divided her time between Paris and New York City. She was an assistant professor of creative writing at San Francisco State University.

TIMOTHY DWIGHT, Yale's eighth president from 1795 to 1817, was the grandson of the great Connecticut-born theologian Jonathan Edwards and the grandfather of Yale's twelfth president, also named Timothy Dwight. The elder Dwight, Massachusetts born, entered Yale at the age of thirteen where he met John Trumbull. During the War for Independence, Dwight served as an army chaplain, and in 1783 he became pastor of a Congregational church in Connecticut, where he remained until appointed president at Yale. His most notable poetic works are *The Conquest of Canaan* (1785), *Greenfield Hill* (1794), and *The Triumph of Infidelity* (1788). Yet his most important writing is *Travels in New England and New York* in four volumes, a valuable source for information about the Northeast at that time (written from notes taken between 1798 and 1808 while touring on horseback, and published in 1821–1822).

RUSSELL EDSON has been called the foremost prose poet in America. Born in Connecticut, Edson's father, a cartoonist, created the character Art Gump. Edson studied the visual arts, but switched to writing in the 1960s. Yet something of the visual and the cartoonist's craft remains in his written work. Since the 1960s he has published many books, including *The Rooster's Wife* and *The Tormented Mirror.* In a letter to Mark Trusi, Edson wrote, "The ideal is to try not to write too much beyond the English articles, a, an, the. I believe, if remembered at all, I'll be remembered for my love of those articles more than any of the matter written between them." In an interview with Trusi, Edson described his writing process as follows: "I sit down to write with a blank page and a blank mind. Wherever the organ of reality (the brain) wants to go I follow with the blue-pencil of consciousness. Poetry is sanity, full brain thinking, where the shape of thought is more important than the particular thought." Edson lives in Stamford, Connecticut.

BRENDAN GALVIN is the author of sixteen volumes of poetry. *Whirl Is King* appeared from LSU Press in 2008. His poems often explore boundaries—those between the sea and the land or those between superstition and science. He taught at Central Connecticut State University from 1969 to 1997, and currently lives in Truro, Massachusetts. He lived for many years in Durham, Connecticut and he was the founder and director of the Connecticut Writers Conference. Galvin told *Contemporary Authors*: "I was accepted at two dental schools, but decided on a master's degree in English, instead. At Northeastern University I took a poetry-writing course with Wallace Stevens scholar Samuel French Morse who encouraged me to try for publication, and in the following year the *Atlantic* accepted two poems." In the spring of 2009 he received the seventh annual Boston College Arts Council Award for Distinguished Achievement.

MARGARET GIBSON is the author of nine volumes of poetry and one prose memoir. *One Body* received a Connecticut Book Award in Poetry, and *Memories of the Future* received the Melville Crane Award. She is professor emerita, University of Connecticut, and lives in Preston, Connecticut. Her meditative poems express a quiet yet precise wonder. As the poet Eamon Grennan has written, "Though never shirking their necessary engagement with the darker truths, Margaret Gibson's poems are always acts of exuberant affirmation."

CHARLOTTE PERKINS GILMAN was born in Hartford, Connecticut, and she was the great-niece of Harriet Beecher Stowe. Gilman grew up in poor and difficult circumstances. Her father abandoned the family, leaving Charlotte's mother, a part-time teacher, to provide for and raise the family. Gilman attended the Rhode Island School of Design where she studied drawing and painting. Although she had vowed never to marry, she married Charles Walter Stetson in 1884. After giving birth to a daughter, she suffered severe depression, left her husband, and moved with her daughter to California. In 1892 she published her famous story "The Yellow Wall-Paper." Although known today for her fiction, Gilman always wrote poetry and in her own time was better known as a poet. She published hundreds of stories and poems and more than a dozen books, including *Women and Economics* (1898). An advocate of euthanasia and diagnosed with inoperable breast cancer, she committed suicide in 1935.

DONALD HALL was born in New Haven, Connecticut. He attended the Bread Loaf Writers' Conference at the age of sixteen and that year had his first work published. His recent volume *White Apples and the Taste of Stone: Selected Poems, 1946–2006* contains work from seven decades. Other volumes of poetry include the moving and affecting volume *Without*, published on the third anniversary of the death of his wife and fellow poet, Jane Kenyon, and *The One Day*, which won the National Book Critics Circle Award and the *Los Angeles Times* Book Prize. Hall has also written memoirs, short stories, children's books, books on baseball, a book on the sculptor Henry Moore, and a book on the poet Marianne Moore. He is well known to college students for the textbook *Writing Well*, now in its ninth edition. He has edited many books, including the well-known poetry anthologies *New Poets of England and America* (with Robert Pack and Louis Simpson) and *Contemporary American Poetry*. He was poetry editor of *The Paris Review* from 1953 to 1962 and a member of the editorial board for poetry at Wesleyan University Press from 1958 to 1964. He also served as editor of the University of Michigan's "Poets on Poetry" series. Hall taught at Michigan for seventeen years. After a campus visit by the writer Robert Graves, Hall decided to follow Graves's advice and forsake college teaching. With the encouragement of Kenyon, he gave up the security of tenure and moved back east to a New Hampshire farmhouse. In the words of poet Liam Rector, Hall, a former United States poet laureate, "has lived deeply within the New England ethos of plain living and high thinking, and he has done so with a sense of humor and eros."

CHARLES O. HARTMAN has taught at Connecticut College since 1984. Currently, he is professor of English, poet-in-residence, co-director of the creative writing program, and chair of the English Department. Hartman is also a jazz guitarist, and he studies computer programming and has used programs to create mixed-media works and to preserve out-of-print poetry. He has published six volumes of poetry and three critical works. The poet David Antin has said that Hartman "is a precisionist of language, an improviser searching familiar scales for a wrong note, a word or phrase, that can take him past regular habits of meaning or melody to some new kind of right place."

JAMES ABRAHAM HILLHOUSE of New Haven was the son of a long-time member of Congress, James Hillhouse, who also served as treasurer of Yale College for fifty years. James Abraham graduated from Yale in 1808 and three years later, upon completing the requirements for a master's degree, he delivered an oration entitled "The Education of a Poet." After brief residences in Boston and New York where he worked to improve his commercial interests, he traveled in Europe and then in 1822 settled into his country seat at New Haven, Sachem's Wood. Here he followed the callings of a man of wealth, leisure, and artistic interests. Among his poetic works are *Percy's Masque*, *Hadad*, *The Judgment*, and *Sachem's Wood*.

JOHN HOLLANDER, born in New York City, is the Sterling Professor Emeritus of English at Yale University and a former poet laureate of the state of Connecticut. He is the author of *A Draft of Light* and seventeen previous books of poetry, including *Picture Window* and *Selected Poetry*. His first book, *A Crackling of Thorns*, was chosen by W. H. Auden as the 1958 volume in the Yale Series of Younger Poets. He has written eight books of criticism, including the award-winning *Rhyme's Reason: A Guide to English Verse* and *The Work of Poetry*. He has received the Bollingen Prize, the Levinson Prize, and the MLA Shaughnessy Medal, among many other awards.

SUSAN HOWE, a long-time resident of Guilford, Connecticut, was born in Boston, Massachusetts. She is a poet-scholar whose writing is deeply rooted in New England history. She received an American Book Award for her critical study *My Emily Dickinson*, and *The Birth-Mark: Unsettling the Wilderness in American Literary History* was named an "International Book of the Year" by the *Times Literary Supplement*. Her many books of poetry include *The Midnight* (a Connecticut Book Award winner) and, most recently, *Souls of the Labadie Tract*. She was the Samuel P. Capen Chair of Poetry and the Humanities at the State University of New York–Buffalo, and she has served as a chancellor of the Academy of American Poets. She began her artistic career as a visual artist, graduating from the Boston Museum School of Fine Arts in 1961 with first prize in painting. Over the next decade she made drawings that included words and then began writing poetry. Her interests lie also in the fields of religion and philosophy, as well as in poetry, place, and history. In 2011 she received the Bollingen Prize for Poetry.

DAVID HUMPHREYS, the son of a Congregational minister, was born in Derby, Connecticut, and attended Yale College where he began his friendship with Trumbull, Dwight, and Barlow. He entered the army at the rank of captain and in 1778 attained the rank of major when he joined the staff of General Putnam. In 1780 he was appointed aide-de-camp to General Washington, and Humphreys's close association with Washington continued after the war. In 1784 he served as secretary to the Franklin, Adams, and Jefferson commission for the negotiation of treaties for foreign commerce. Humphreys served next in the Connecticut state legislature and then for a period of years as a diplomat to Portugal and Spain. He is sometimes called "America's first diplomat," though he often called himself Colonel Humphreys, referring to his military rank. Upon return to Connecticut he encouraged advancements in manufacturing and agriculture. He brought merino sheep from Spain back to Connecticut and is hence considered the founder of the woolen industry in America. The Humphreys House is now the headquarters of the Derby Historical Society and open every weekday from one to four.

GRAY JACOBIK is a professor emerita at Eastern Connecticut State University. She lives in Deep River, Connecticut, and has until recently been on the poetry faculty at the Stonecoast MFA in creative writing program. She is a recipient of fellowships from the National Endowment for the Arts and the Connecticut Commission on the Arts. She is an accomplished painter as well as poet. Her most recent book is a memoir in verse titled *Little Boy Blue*. Jacobik has said that she is "a poet whose purpose in life is to pass on what she knows." More particularly, she has said, "the poetry that matters most to me is written, as Yeats would have it, 'in the rag-and-bone shop of the heart.'"

JAMES LAUGHLIN, founder and publisher of New Directions, died in 1997 at the age of eighty-three while on his way from his home in Norfolk, Connecticut, to the hospital in Sharon. After his early years in Pittsburgh, Pennsylvania, Laughlin attended The Choate School in Wallingford, Connecticut. He attended Harvard but found himself bored by professors who had little interest in contemporary letters, so he set out for Europe to meet and learn from the contemporary masters first hand. He studied for several months at the Ezuversity, the home of Ezra Pound in Rapallo, Italy. Pound, who told Laughlin that he would never amount to much as a poet, offered some advice: return to America, he said, put your life and the family steel fortune to good use and start a publishing company. Laughlin did. In 1936 he started New Directions in Norfolk, Connecticut, a literary press that would become one of the most important institutions for the art of writing in the twentieth century. New Directions served as the primary publisher for William Carlos Williams, Thomas Merton, Tennessee Williams, Gary Snyder, Denise Levertov, John Hawkes, and Susan Howe, as well as Pound. And despite Pound's harsh words, Laughlin continued to write poetry and, late in life, published much of it. His poetic work is at times casual and other times formal. He could be at times very humorous and at others elegiac. He wrote in epigrams and in long form. *Byways*, Laughlin's long autobiographical poem left unfinished at his death and published by New Directions in 2005, recalls not only much of his family life and literary friendships, but also the terse poetic form that he favored in his own writing.

J. D. MCCLATCHY was born in Bryn Mawr, Pennsylvania, and educated at Georgetown and Yale. In 2000 he received the Connecticut Governor's Arts Award. His impressive and varied literary arts career has resulted in copious editing, prolific opera libretti composition, and essay writing as well as the publication of six volumes of poems. Among his editing projects are James Merrill's *Selected Poems*, *Poets of the Civil War*, and *Bright Pages: Yale Writers 1701–2001*. He has written more than a dozen opera libretti for composers such as Ned Rorem, William Schuman, and Lorin Maazel, with productions at La Scala, Lincoln Center, and by the Chicago Lyric Opera. His essays have been collected in *White Paper* (1989) and *Twenty Questions* (1998). In 2009 he was elected president of the American Academy of Arts and Letters. He is professor of English at Yale, editor of *The Yale Review*, and lives in Stonington, Connecticut.

WILLIAM MEREDITH taught at Connecticut College for nearly thirty years. He was born in New York City and graduated from Princeton. He worked briefly for *The New York Times* before entering the armed services where he became a carrier pilot in the United States Navy. In 1944, Archibald MacLeish chose Meredith's first volume of poetry, *Love Letter from an Impossible Land*, for the Yale Series of Younger Poets. Meredith re-entered the navy as a pilot in the Korean War and achieved the rank of lieutenant commander. His poetry received the National Book Award, the *Los Angeles Times* Book Award, and the Pulitzer Prize. He also worked as an editor and translator, editing *Poets of Bulgaria* and translating Guillaume Apollinaire's *Alcools*. For several years, he and his partner, Richard Harteis, divided their time between Connecticut and Bulgaria. Michael Collier, a former student of Meredith's, wrote in his foreword to Meredith's *Effort at Speech: New and Selected Poems* (1997): "In 1983, at the age of sixty-four, William Meredith suffered a stroke that left him with expressive aphasia, which means that for the past fourteen years he has not been able to use language to say or write exactly what he wants to say [. . .] Trapped, as it were, inside his body, which has profoundly betrayed him, for the past decade and a half Meredith has remained occupied with the poet's struggle—the struggle to speak." William Meredith died in

2007 in New London, Connecticut. His papers are housed at the Connecticut College Library, and Riverrun, his home on the Thames River in Connecticut for sixty years, is a state of Connecticut historic landmark managed by the William Meredith Foundation.

JAMES MERRILL won the National Book Award in poetry for *Nights and Days*. Other books and awards include the Bollingen Prize for *Braving the Elements*, the Pulitzer Prize for *Divine Comedies*, another National Book Award for *Mirabell*, the National Book Critics Circle Award for his epic *The Changing Light at Sandover*, and the Bobbitt National Prize awarded by the Library of Congress for *The Inner Room*. From 1955 until his death in 1995, he and his partner David Jackson maintained a residence in Stonington, Connecticut. This small coastal town inspired some of Merrill's most important work, including the volumes *Water Street* and *The Changing Light at Sandover*. Merrill left 107 Water Street to the town. The Stonington Village Improvement Association has kept the home intact and has opened it as a place for writers and scholars to live and work. Merrill was also the first and longest serving poet laureate of Connecticut, from 1985 to 1995.

MARILYN NELSON, born in Cleveland, Ohio, into a military family that frequently moved, began teaching at the University of Connecticut in 1978 and is now a professor emeritus of English at UConn. She served as poet laureate of Connecticut from 2001 to 2006. She is also a Connecticut Book Award recipient, having received the award for both poetry and children's literature in 2002 for *Carver: A Life in Poems*. While her father, an air force pilot, provided, as Nelson put it, "wings," her mother, a history teacher, provided "roots." Nelson has written several book-length poetry sequences for young readers inspired by events in American history, most recently *The Freedom Business*, about Venture Smith, a Connecticut slave whose personal account was first published in 1798. Nelson has also worked to further the art of poetry in the present as well as writing poetry to honor the past. Most notably, she is founder and director of Soul Mountain Retreat, a small writers' colony in Connecticut. Upon receiving the 2006 Connecticut Center for the Book Lifetime Achievement Award, she said that she felt she was "getting an award for breathing—for something I could not not do." Among her books are *The Fields of Praise: New and Selected Poems* (1997) and *Sweethearts of Rhythm* (2009).

CHARLES OLSON, born in Worcester, Massachusetts, received his bachelor's and master's degrees at Wesleyan University in 1932 and 1933, respectively. While at Wesleyan he began a study of Herman Melville that would be published in 1947 as *Call Me Ishmael*, a classic work of American literary studies in the tradition of William Carlos Williams's *In the American Grain* and a predecessor of Susan Howe's *My Emily Dickinson*. Between the early '30s and late '40s, Olson pursued, but did not complete, a doctorate at Harvard and worked for New Deal programs and the Democratic Party. He did not publish poems until his mid-thirties, but from that time forward he devoted his life to poetry and abandoned the political sphere. He had great influence on many poets in the '50s, '60s, and '70s through his lectures and essays, as well as by virtue of the example of his own poems, especially his epic, *Maximus*. In "Projective Verse" (1950), he stated, "A poem is energy transferred from where the poet got it (he will have some several causations), by way of the poem itself to, all the way over to, the reader," and in "Human Universe" (1951) he warned, "All individual energy and ingenuity is bought off—at a suggestion box or at the cinema. Passivity conquers all." He served as rector of Black Mountain College during its fervent final years, a small but vital center of artistic energy in post-war America. He lived in Gloucester, Massachusetts, until he took a teaching post at the State University of New York at Buffalo; thereafter, he taught briefly at the University of Connecticut before succumbing to cancer. The Thomas J. Dodd Research Center at Connecticut houses the Charles Olson Research Collection.

F. D. REEVE (Franklin D'Olier) has said that the key person in his life as a poet was R. P. Blackmur "from whom I learned that the reading and writing of books was a respectable, indeed, a preferable, highly valuable alternative to the middle-class, business-and-banking careers of my conservative family." In addition to being an inspiring teacher, Blackmur also introduced Reeve at his first important New York poetry reading, which took place at the 92nd Street Y in the company of Denise Levertov and Daniel Berrigan. Reeve also had a close relationship with Robert Frost, whom he accompanied on a famous State Department–sponsored trip to the Soviet Union in 1962. Reeve taught for many years at Wesleyan University and became close friends of writers Paul Horgan and William Meredith. Though he eventually made Vermont his permanent home, he did live for a time in Higganum, Connecticut, and served as a member of the Haddam Democratic Town Committee. He is the author of many volumes of poetry and several works of fiction. He is a well-known translator of modern Russian writing and has also edited several collections of Russian literature. His nonfiction writings include *Robert Frost in Russia* and *The Russian Novel*. In an essay entitled "Literary Place," he wrote: "As we read, the real and the imagined places become ours. Indeed, the poems themselves would be inconceivable without their relief maps of emotions, for our most intense emotions are always tied to some person, some place." Reeve is married to novelist Laura Stevenson.

VIVIAN SHIPLEY, Connecticut State University Distinguished Professor and editor of the *Connecticut Review*, lives in North Haven, Connecticut. She is the author of nine books of poetry, including *All of Your Messages Have Been Erased*. In 2003 she received the Connecticut Book Award in Poetry for *When There Is No Shore* and in 2005 she received the Lifetime Achievement Award from the Connecticut Center for the Book. Raised in Kentucky, she is a member of the University of Kentucky Hall of Distinguished Alumni. Shipley often writes about family relationships and the landscapes within which these relationships exist—be it rural farmland in Kentucky or the suburbanized shoreline of Connecticut.

LYDIA SIGOURNEY, born in Norwich, Connecticut, the only child of a gardener-handyman and his wife, became one of the most popular and financially successful writers in nineteenth-century America. After several years of teaching in Hartford, she gave up her employment upon her engagement to the local wealthy businessman Charles Sigourney. Her book *Moral Pieces in Prose and Verse* had already been published at the instigation and expense of the art patron Daniel Wadsworth. She would follow this publication with approximately fifty books, mostly poems, but also prose works such as *Connecticut Forty Years Since* and advice books such as *Letters to Young Ladies*. Her husband at first discouraged her writing, but when his fortunes declined, he became more acquiescent to his wife's writing career.

WALLACE STEVENS, born in Reading, Pennsylvania, educated at Harvard and New York Law School, was associated with the Hartford Accident & Indemnity Company beginning in 1916, and from 1934 until his death he served as vice president. A master of exquisite verse, Stevens was specifically concerned with creating some shape or order in the "slovenly wilderness" of chaos. His volumes of poetry include *Harmonium* (1923), *Ideas of Order* (1936), *The Man with the Blue Guitar* (1937), *Parts of a World* (1942), *Transport to Summer* (1947), *The Auroras of Autumn* (1950), and *Collected Poems* (1954). The latter work received both the Pulitzer Prize in Poetry and the National Book Award in Poetry. In June 2009 The Hartford Friends and Enemies of Wallace Stevens dedicated the 2.4-mile Wallace Stevens Walk, a tribute to the poet that traces his walk from his office to his home, marked by thirteen Stony Creek, Connecticut, granite markers, each inscribed with a stanza of "Thirteen Ways of Looking at a Blackbird." In a letter from December 1932, Stevens wrote: "We bought a house some time ago out on Westerly Terrace, which is a twig running off from Terry Road, which, you may remember, is a branch running off the main stem of Asylum Avenue. Without launching into any description of the house (which, I suppose, is very much like other houses), it is enough to say that we are delighted with it, although a little short of furniture."

HARRIET BEECHER STOWE published more than thirty books in her lifetime, including her antislavery novel *Uncle Tom's Cabin* (1852). She also wrote advice books, books for children, biographies, and poetry. Her poems are often devoutly religious. She was the daughter of one preacher and the wife of another. She grew up in Litchfield, Connecticut, and recalls childhood events in her novel *Poganuc People* (1878). She wrote for more than fifty years and did so to make money as well as to right wrongs and improve society. The Stowes maintained a primary residence in Hartford for more than thirty years. Their home, now called the Harriet Beecher Stowe Center, a brick Gothic cottage on Forest Street, can be visited today.

JOHN TRUMBULL entered Yale at the age of thirteen. He dedicated his early years to Yale, serving as a tutor and advocating for a broader curriculum. In 1772, Trumbull published the first part of his satire on contemporary education, *The Progress of Dulness*. The following year he turned his attention to law and entered the office of John Adams in Boston. As war approached he returned to Connecticut. He wrote poems and essays in support of the cause of liberty, including his second lengthy satire *M'Fingal*. Rev. Charles W. Everest, writing in the 1840s, called this poem "a merciless satire, directed by a powerful hand, and with an unerring aim." After independence Trumbull settled in Hartford and participated in a literary club along with David Humphreys, Joel Barlow, and Lemuel Hopkins. Trumbull served in the state legislature and in various judicial posts for the state of Connecticut. From 1825 until his death in 1831 he lived with his daughter and her family in Detroit.

LEWIS TURCO once said that although he lived almost forty years of his life near the Great Lakes, "the fourteen years in Meriden, [. . .] and the four spent in the Navy just after my graduation from Meriden High in 1952—two of them aboard the *Hornet*—were the seminal years, for they saw me begin my career as a writer." After his service in the navy, Turco returned to Connecticut and graduated from the University of Connecticut before attending the Writers Workshop at the University of Iowa. Founding director of both the Cleveland State University Poetry Center and the Program in Writing Arts at the State University of New York at Oswego, he published his classic *The Book of Forms: A Handbook of Poetics* in 1968. His formal verse poems are published in *The Collected Lyrics of Lewis Turco / Wesli Court, 1953–2004* and *The Gathering of the Elders*, while *Fearful Pleasures: The Complete Poems, 1959–2007* contains the non-formal poems published in a dozen previous volumes.

CHASE TWICHELL was born in New Haven, Connecticut, and graduated from Trinity College in Hartford before earning an MFA from the University of Iowa. She has worked as an editor for the Pennyroyal Press and the University of Alabama Press. In 1999 she founded Ausable Press. She also co-edited with Robin Behn *The Practice of Poetry: Writing Exercises from Poets Who Teach*. Twichell's most recent volume of poetry, *Horses Where the Answers Should Have Been*, provides generous selections from six previous books, 1981–2005, and twenty-seven new poems (in a sense a seventh book). *Horses Where the Answers Should Have Been* shows Twichell to be an ever-dark, deep, sonorous, and serious voice.

MARK VAN DOREN taught at Columbia University from 1920 to 1959. During that time he inspired many future poets including Louis Simpson, Richard Howard, John Hollander, John Berryman, Thomas Merton, and Allen Ginsberg. In his autobiography Thomas Merton recalls a class he took at Columbia taught by Van Doren: "Most of the time he asked questions. His questions were very good, and if you tried to answer them intelligently, you found yourself saying excellent things that you did not know you knew, and that you had not, in fact, known before." Today the Columbia award for excellence in teaching bears the name the Mark Van Doren Award. Van Doren split his time between New York City and his rural retreat in Cornwall, Connecticut. He was an editor and biographer as well as a poet, professor, and scholar. His *Collected Poems* (1939) received a Pulitzer Prize. He died in Torrington, Connecticut, on December 10, 1972.

ROBERT PENN WARREN was born in Guthrie, Kentucky, and educated at Vanderbilt, the University of California, Yale, and Oxford. He taught at Yale and lived for many years in Fairfield, Connecticut. As a young man he belonged to the regional group of poets known as the Southern Agrarians or Fugitives, and although he began his career as a poet, he also became a well-known novelist and scholar. Among his volumes of verse are *Brother to Dragons* and *Audubon: A Vision*; among his novels are *Night Rider* and *All the King's Men*. As a scholar he collaborated with Cleanth Brooks on the influential textbooks *Understanding Poetry* and *Understanding Fiction*. Warren received three Pulitzer Prizes for his writing and many other distinctions, including being named in 1986 the first United States poet laureate.

ROSANNA WARREN, daughter of Robert Penn Warren and Eleanor Clark, was born in Fairfield, Connecticut, grew up in Redding, and studied painting at Yale University, where she graduated in 1976. She received her master's from The Writing Seminars at Johns Hopkins University. Since completing her education, she has published five volumes of poetry, a translation of Euripides's *Suppliant Women* (with Stephen Scully), a book of literary criticism, and several edited books, including *The Art of Translation: Voices from the Field*. In the preface to *Fables of the Self: Studies in Lyric Poetry*, she wrote: "I grew up in a literary family; by what I think of as an accident of biology, my parents were well-known writers. As a young person in love with stories and poems from an early age, I came to struggle with the self-consciousness induced by a growing sense of literature as the parental preserve. For years, I tried to be a painter, and kept my writing private." Among the awards she has received are the May Sarton Prize and the Ingram Merrill Foundation Award. In 2004 the American Academy of Arts and Letters granted her the Award of Merit in Poetry, given once every six years to an outstanding poet. Warren served as chancellor of the Academy of American Poets from 1999 to 2005, and she is the Emma MacLachlan Metcalf Professor of the Humanities at Boston University, where she has received distinction for excellence in teaching.

RICHARD WILBUR was born in New York City. He attended Amherst College and then served in the United States Army during World War II. He then studied at Harvard and began his long career as a poet, translator, and esteemed man of letters. His 2004 *Collected Poems* contains the writing of slightly more than sixty years. In introducing this volume, Wilbur wrote,

"I once asked Wallace Stevens whether he liked such-and-such a poem of his, and he heartily replied, 'I like *all* my poems.' Every poet has moments of feeling that way, moved by gratitude for all the times when he got something decently said, or hoped to have done so, and could in conscience add another poem to his manuscript." Wilbur's "manuscript" is remarkable, indeed. He wrote the lyrics that accompany Leonard Bernstein's music for the hit show *Candide*; he drew the clever and comic illustrations for his books geared to children; his translations of Molière and Racine set the standard. He has received two Pulitzer Prizes, a National Book Award, the Wallace Stevens Award, two Bollingen Prizes, two PEN translation awards, and many other honors. He is a former poet laureate of the United States and taught for many years at Wesleyan University in Middletown, Connecticut, beginning in 1957.

Publications and Credits

Elizabeth Alexander: "Tina Green," "Ars Poetica #92: Marcus Garvey on Elocution," "Connecticut," and "The *Amistad* Trail" from *Crave Radiance: New and Selected Poems 1990–2010*. Copyright © 2011 by Elizabeth Alexander. Reprinted with the permission of The Permissions Company, Inc. on behalf of Graywolf Press, Minneapolis, Minnesota, www.graywolfpress.org.

Dick Allen: "Foreword" used by permission of the author; "Another Knowledge," "On The New Haven Line," "To A Woman Half A World Away," "A Last Memory of Korea," and "The Persistence" copyright © 1997 by Dick Allen, from *Ode to the Cold War: Poems New and Selected*, published by Sarabande Books. Used by permission of the author.

Doug Anderson: "First Blood" copyright © 1994 by Doug Anderson, from *The Moon Reflected Fire*, published by Alice James Books; "History Blues," "The Oracle," and "Crows" copyright 2000 by Doug Anderson, from *Blues for Unemployed Secret Police*, published by Curbstone Press. Used by permission of the author.

Sophie Cabot Black: "Lost," "The Harrowing," "The Climb," and "Threshold" from *The Descent*. Copyright © 2004 by Sophie Cabot Black. Reprinted with the permission of The Permissions Company, Inc. on behalf of Graywolf Press, Minneapolis, Minnesota, www.graywolfpress. org.

George F. Butterick: "1970," "The Walker," "Gurleyville Road," and "The Distances," from *The Collected Poems of George F. Butterick*, published by The Poetry / Rare Books Collection, SUNY Buffalo in 1988. Reprinted with the permission of the Literary Estate of George F. Butterick.

Gabrielle Calvocoressi: "The Death of Towns" and "Late Twentieth Century in the Form of Litany," from *The Last Time I Saw Amelia Earhart* and *Apocalyptic Swing: Poems* copyright © 2005, 2009 by Gabrielle Calvocoressi. Reprinted by permission of Persea Books, Inc., New York.

Hayden Carruth: "The Sound of Snow" and "Stepping Backward," from *Collected Shorter Poems 1946–1991*. Copyright © 1959, 1974, 1992 by Hayden Carruth. "The Mythology of Dark and Light," from *Collected Longer Poems*. Copyright © 1971, 1994 by Hayden Carruth. Reprinted with the permission of The Permissions Company, Inc. on behalf of Copper Canyon Press, www.coppercanyonpress.org.

Richard Deming: "OH," "Wintering the Turn," "Annus Mirabilis," and "Mise En Scene" copyright © 2007 by Richard Deming, from *Let's Not Call It Consequence*, published by Shearsman Books. Used by permission of the author.

Stacy Doris: selection from *Knot* copyright © 2006 by Stacy Doris, published by the University of Georgia Press; selection from *Cheerleader's Guide to the World: Council Book* copyright © 2006 by Stacy Doris, published by Roof Books. Used by permission of the author.

Russell Edson: "A Chair," "A Stone Is Nobody's," "The Ancestral Mousetrap," "The Ceremony," and "The Matter" copyright © 1994 by Russell Edson, from *The Tunnel: Selected Poems*, published by Oberlin College Press. Used by permission of the author.

Brendan Galvin: "The Potatoes Have a Word to Say," "The Connecticut River in Flood," and excerpt from "Wampanoag Traveler" copyright © 2005 by Brendan Galvin, from *Habitat: New and Selected Poems, 1965–2005*, published by the Louisiana State University Press. Used by permission of the author.

Margaret Gibson: "A Ripple of Deer, A Metamorphosis of Bear, A Metaphor of Mountains" copyright © 1989 by Margaret Gibson, from *Out in the Open*, published by the Louisiana State University Press; "Elegy for a Dancer" and "Icon" (pages 96–98) copyright © 2001 by Margaret Gibson, from *Icon and Evidence*, published by the Louisiana State University Press; "Newspaper Photograph" copyright © 2007 by Margaret Gibson, from *One Body*, published by the Louisiana State University Press. Used by permission of the author and the publisher.

Donald Hall: "Christmas Eve in Whitneyville," "White Apples," "1943," and "Kicking the Leaves" from *White Apples and the Taste of Stone: Selected Poems, 1946–2006* by Donald Hall. Copyright © 2006 by Donald Hall. Reprinted by permission of Houghton Mifflin Harcourt Publishing Company. All rights reserved.

Charles O. Hartman: "Petting Zoo," "A Walk in Winter," and "Tuxedo" copyright © 2008 by Charles O. Hartman, from *New & Selected Poems*, published by Ahsahta Press. Used by permission of the author.

John Hollander: "An Old Song," "Pageant of the Cold," "That's for Oblivion," "Collected Novels," and "Adam's Task" copyright © 1993 by John Hollander, from *Selected Poetry*, published by Alfred A. Knopf. Used by permission of the author.

Susan Howe: "Silence Wager Stories" copyright © 1993 by Susan Howe, from *The Nonconformist's Memorial*, published by New Directions. Used by permission of the author.

Gray Jacobik: "Skirts," "The Wooden Egg," and "The Banquet" copyright © 1998 by Gray Jacobik, from *The Double Task*, published by the University of Massachusetts Press; "Of Cos Cob in Snow" copyright © 2002 by Gray Jacobik, from *Brave Disguises*, published by the University of Pittsburgh Press. Used by permission of the author.

James Laughlin: "Is Memory" and "What the Pencil Writes," from *Poems New and Selected*, copyright © 1995 by James Laughlin. Reprinted by permission of New Directions Publishing Corp. "My Aunt," from *Byways*, copyright © 1994 by James Laughlin. Reprinted by permission of New Directions Publishing Corp. "The Old Men," from *The Country Road*, copyright © 1993 by James Laughlin. Reprinted by permission of New Directions Publishing Corp.

J. D. McClatchy: "Late Autumn Walk" copyright © 1981 by J. D. McClatchy, from *Scenes from Another Life*, published by George Braziller. Used by permission of the author. "The Bookcase" from *Hazmat: Poems* by J. D. McClatchy, copyright © 2002 by J. D. McClatchy. Used by permission of Alfred A. Knopf, a division of Random House, Inc. "E R" from *Mercury Dressing: Poems* by J. D. McClatchy, copyright © 2009 by J. D. McClatchy. Used by permission of Alfred A. Knopf, a division of Random House, Inc.

William Meredith: "The Open Sea," "The Wreck of the Thresher," "Winter Verse for His Sister," and "Here and There" are reprinted from *Effort at Speech: New and Selected Poems* by William Meredith, published by TriQuarterly Books/Northwestern University Press in 1997. Copyright © 1997 by William Meredith. All rights reserved; used by permission of Northwestern University Press and Richard Harteis.

James Merrill: "A Tenancy," "The Emerald," "The Victor Dog," and "Dead Center" from *Collected Poems* by James Merrill, edited by J. D. McClatchy and Stephen Yenser, copyright © 2001 by the Literary Estate of James Merrill at Washington University. Used by permission of Alfred A. Knopf, a division of Random House, Inc. Excerpt from "Mirabell: Books of Number" from *The Changing Light at Sandover* by James Merrill, copyright © 1980, 1982 by James Merrill. Used by permission of Alfred A. Knopf, a division of Random House, Inc.

Marilyn Nelson: "Churchgoing," "Sisters," "Juneteenth," and "Psalm" copyright © 1997 by Marilyn Nelson, from *The Fields of Praise: New and Selected Poems*, published by the Louisiana State University Press. Used by permission of the author.

Charles Olson: Excerpt from "As the Dead Prey upon Us" and "Variations Done for Gerald Van De Wiele," from *Selected Writings*, copyright © 1966 by Charles Olson. Reprinted by permission of New Directions Publishing Corp.

F. D. Reeve: "Night River" copyright © 1968 by F. D. Reeve, from *In the Silent Stones*, published by William Morrow; "Identity Crisis" copyright © 1972 by F. D. Reeve, from *The Blue Cat*, published by Farrar, Straus, Giroux; "Watersong" copyright © 2001 by F. D. Reeve, from *The Urban Stampede and Other Poems*, published by the Michigan State University Press; "what the cranes said" copyright © 2006 by F. D. Reeve, from *The Toy Soldier and Other Poems*, published by Bayeux Arts. Used by permission of the author.

Vivian Shipley: "Moonflower" copyright © 1999 by Vivian Shipley, from *Crazy Quilt*, published by Hanover Press; "Digging Up Peonies" copyright © 2000 by Vivian Shipley, from *Fair Haven*, published by Negative Capability Press; "Static Holds a Grudge" and "Number Fifty-two: Winifred Benham, Hartford, Connecticut, October 7, 1697" copyright © 2002 by Vivian Shipley, from *When There Is No Shore*, published by Word Press. Used by permission of the author.

Wallace Stevens: "Of Hartford in a Purple Light," excerpt from "An Ordinary Evening in New Haven," "The Plain Sense of Things," and "The River of Rivers in Connecticut" from *The Collected Poems of Wallace Stevens* by Wallace Stevens, copyright © 1954 by Wallace Stevens and renewed 1982 by Holly Stevens. Used by permission of Alfred A. Knopf, a division of Random House, Inc.

Lewis Turco: "Ode on St. Cecilia's Day 1964," "The Late, Late Show," "The Recurring Dream," and "Wake Disturbing Surfaces" copyright © 2007 by Lewis Turco, from *Fearful Pleasures: The Complete Poems 1959–2007*, published by Star Cloud Press. Used by permission of the author and the publisher.

Chase Twichell: "Why All Good Music Is Sad," "The Paper River," and "Savin Rock" copyright © 2010 by Chase Twichell, from *Horses Where the Answers Should Have Been: New and Selected Poems*, published by Copper Canyon Press. Used by permission of the author.

Mark Van Doren: "Going Home," "The Unknown Army," "The Seven Sleepers," and "Anger in the Room." Used by permission.

Robert Penn Warren: "Small White House," copyright 1976 by Robert Penn Warren; "Evening Hawk," copyright © 1985 by Robert Penn Warren; "Rather Like a Dream" and "Heart of Autumn," copyright © 1978 by Robert Penn Warren. Used by permission.

Rosanna Warren: "Orchard," "Snow," and "World Trade Center," from *Each Leaf Shines*

Separate by Rosanna Warren. Copyright © 1984 by Rosanna Warren. Used by permission of W. W. Norton & Company, Inc. "Day Lilies," from *Departure: Poems* by Rosanna Warren. Copyright © 2003 by Rosanna Warren. Used by permission of W. W. Norton & Company, Inc.

Richard Wilbur: "In Trackless Woods" from *Collected Poems: 1943–2004*. Copyright © 2004 by Richard Wilbur; reprinted by permission of Houghton Mifflin Harcourt Publishing Company. "In the Field" from *Walking to Sleep: New Poems and Translations*. Copyright © 1968 and renewed 1996 by Richard Wilbur; reprinted by permission of Houghton Mifflin Harcourt Publishing Company. (Originally appeared in *The New Yorker*.) "Advice to a Prophet" from *Advice to a Prophet and Other Poems*. Copyright © 1959 and renewed 1987 by Richard Wilbur; reprinted by permission of Houghton Mifflin Harcourt Publishing Company. "A World Without Objects Is a Sensible Emptiness" from *Ceremony and Other Poems* copyright © 1950 and renewed 1978 by Richard Wilbur; reprinted by permission of Houghton Mifflin Harcourt Publishing Company. "The Beautiful Changes" from *The Beautiful Changes and Other Poems*, copyright © 1947 and renewed 1975 by Richard Wilbur; reprinted by permission of Houghton Mifflin Harcourt Publishing Company.

Index of Titles

Garnet Books

Garnet Poems:
An Anthology of Connecticut Poetry Since 1776
Edited by Dennis Barone

Food for the Dead:
On the Trail of New England's Vampires
by Michael E. Bell

Early Connecticut Silver, 1700–1840
by Peter Bohan and Philip Hammerslough
Introduction and Notes by Erin Eisenbarth

The Connecticut River:
A Photographic Journey through the Heart of New England
by Al Braden

Connecticut's Fife & Drum Tradition
by James Clark

Sunken Garden Poetry, 1992–2011
Edited by Brad Davis

The Old Leather Man:
Historical Accounts of a Connecticut and New York Legend
by Daniel DeLuca

Post Roads & Iron Horses:
Transportation in Connecticut from Colonial Times to the Age of Steam
by Richard DeLuca

Dr. Mel's Connecticut Climate Book
by Dr. Mel Goldstein

Hidden in Plain Sight:
A Deep Traveler Explores Connecticut
by David K. Leff

Westover School:
Giving Girls a Place of Their Own
by Laurie Lisle

Crowbar Governor:
The Life and Times of Morgan Gardner Bulkeley
by Kevin Murphy

Fly Fishing in Connecticut:
A Guide for Beginners
by Kevin Murphy

Water for Hartford:
The Story of the Hartford Water Works and the Metropolitan District Commission
by Kevin Murphy

Henry Austin:
In Every Variety of Architectural Style
by James F. O'Gorman

Ella Grasso:
Connecticut's Pioneering Governor
by Jon E. Purmont

Making Freedom:
The Extraordinary Life of Venture Smith
by Chandler B. Saint and George Krimsky

Welcome to Wesleyan:
Campus Buildings
by Leslie Starr

Gervase Wheeler:
A British Architect in America, 1847–1860
by Renée Tribert and James F. O'Gorman

Connecticut in the American Civil War:
Slavery, Sacrifice, and Survival
by Matthew Warshauer

Stories in Stone:
How Geology Influenced Connecticut History and Culture
by Jelle Zeilinga de Boer

About the Editor

DENNIS BARONE (1955–) has taught at the University of Saint Joseph (formerly Saint Joseph College) in West Hartford, Connecticut, since 1986. He grew up in Teaneck and Ramsey, New Jersey, graduated from Bard College and received his master's and doctoral degrees from the University of Pennsylvania. He is author or editor of twenty-one books, including as author *Field Report* (stories) and *Parallel Lines* (poetry) and as editor *New Hungers for Old: One-Hundred Years of Italian-American Poetry.*

About the Driftless Connecticut Series

The Driftless Connecticut Series is a publication award program established in 2010 to recognize excellent books with a Connecticut focus or written by a Connecticut author. To be eligible, the book must have a Connecticut topic or setting or an author must have been born in Connecticut or have been a legal resident of Connecticut for at least three years.

The Driftless Connecticut Series is funded by the Beatrice Fox Auerbach Foundation Fund at the Hartford Foundation for Public Giving. For more information and a complete list of books in the Driftless Connecticut Series, please visit us online at http://www.wesleyan.edu/wespress/driftless.